Hampshire Poets
Edited by Mark Richardson

First published in Great Britain in 2010 by

Remus House
Coltsfoot Drive
Peterborough
PE2 9JX
Telephone: 01733 890066
Website: www.youngwriters.co.uk

All Rights Reserved
Book Design by Spencer Hart
© Copyright Contributors 2009
SB ISBN 978-1-84924-792-4

Foreword

At Young Writers our defining aim is to promote an enjoyment of reading and writing amongst children and young adults. By giving aspiring poets the opportunity to see their work in print, their love of the written word as well as confidence in their own abilities has the chance to blossom.

Our latest competition Poetry Explorers was designed to introduce primary school children to the wonders of creative expression. They were given free reign to write on any theme and in any style, thus encouraging them to use and explore a variety of different poetic forms.

We are proud to present the resulting collection of regional anthologies which are an excellent showcase of young writing talent. With such a diverse range of entries received, the selection process was difficult yet very rewarding. From comical rhymes to poignant verses, there is plenty to entertain and inspire within these pages. We hope you agree that this collection bursting with imagination is one to treasure.

Contents

Beechwood Junior School
Ashton Crosby (10) 1
Lauren Grant (9) 1
Hannah Olivia Price (10) 2
Sophie Stirrat (9) 2
Shani Lambert (7) 3
Kayleigh Barnes (7) 3
Hollie Chapman (9) 3

Bosmere Junior School
Charlotte Remnant (10) 4
Skye Palmer (10) 4
Georgie Donnelly (10) 5
Darcy Matthews (11) 5
Chloe Bradbury (10) 6
Rebecca Simes (10) 6
Rebekah Wells (11) 7
Erin Offord (10) 7
Sasha Harris (10) 8
Toby Andrew Morton (10) 8
Rebecca Ede-Jones (10) 9
Sharna Capel-Watson (10) 9
Rebecca Meades (10) 10

Corpus Christi Primary School
Kaitlan-Pfeiffer-Richardson (9) 10
Charis Almond (9) 11
Rebecca Galbraith (9) 12
Lydia Weedon (9) 13
Olivia Powell (9) 14
Taylor Shawyer 14
Maddison Ferguson (9) 15
Rachael Butler (9) 15
Elise Sherwin (9) 16
Natty Haywood (9) 16
Ben Bramley 17
Ollie Conaghan (9) 17
Leah Cox (10) 18

Dylan Bridle (9) 18
Angela De La Fuente (9) 19
Liya Shaji (9) 19
Laura Smith (9) 20
Rachel Preston (9) 20
Leah Clements (9) 21
Ethan Barker 21

Elson Junior School
Megan Bourne (10) 22
Emma Charleston (8) 23
Emma Cains (9) 23
Emily Chandler (10) 24
Annasley Sheen (9) 24
Hazel Camburn (8) 25
Kelsey Barnes (9) 25
Chelsi Reed (8) 26
Ellodie Beale (9) 26
Rhiannon Smith (9) 27
Eden Heath (9) 27
Taylor Campion (9) 28
Jade Sheppard (10) 28
Leah Robinson (9) 29
Rachel Tapp (7) 29
Erin Tanner (8) 29
Thea Hogg (9) 30
Alegria Tracey (7) 30
Millie Murtagh (9) 30
Alefiya Khedapa (7) 31

Forres Sandle Manor School
Matilda Everard (10) 31
Rosie Landon (10) 32
Freddie Skeates (10) 33
Alice Risebrow (10) 34
Joe Cox (11) 34
Georgia Downes (11) 35
Teddie Pressland (10) 35

Rupert Talfourd-Cook (10) 36
Laurie Smith (10) 36
Olivia Peters 37
Oscar Roberts (10) 37
Jessica Davies (10) 38
Poppy Bolton Carter (10) 38
Ella Rowe (10) 39
William Hall (10) 39
Hannah Fearon (10) 40
Charlie Savage (10) 40
Laura Wyles (10) 41
Alexander Brown (10) 41
Hugo Campbell-Smith (11) 42
Bella Skeates (10) 42
Luke Robinson (10) 43
Samuel Everard (10) 43
Theresa Allsopp (10) 43

Grey House Preparatory School
William Parsons (10) 44
Jonathan Boyce (10) 45
Oliver Amatt (10) 45
Benjamin Amatt (10) 46
Robert Cootes (10) 46
Alisha Windeatt (8) 47
Reuben Chasey (10) 47
Gemma Bertuzzi-Glover (10) 48
Joseph Allen (10) 48
Amy Gower-Jones (8) 49
Anoushka Chandler (10) 49
Timmy Galloway (10) 50
Alex Fraser (10) 50
Sophia Dugdale (10) 51
Jannik Mackel (11) 51
Rosie Hudson (8) 52
Ross Bandeira (9) 52
Sophie Fowles (8) 53
Alexander Polydorou (10) 53
George Griffiths (8) 54
Isobel Warren (8) 54
Keturah Bate (8) 55
Oscar Sutherland Dee (10) 55
Ellen Wilkins (10) 55

Ben Spratley (9) 56
Amanda Clark (8) 56
William Loten (10) 56
Angus Carver (10) 57

Heathfield Junior School
Daisy Folland (10) 57
Nicholas David Donaldson (11) 58
Connor Regan (9) 58
Matilda Tearle (10) 59
Jack Gould (10) 59
Elishia Robinson (11) 60
Kieran Baker (11) 60
Jessica James (9) 61
Faith Parr (8) 61
Jack Wilson (10) 62
Callum Wolfe (10) 62
Kevin Chung (9) 63
Rhonwen Ellis (8) 63
Samantha Bridle (10) 64
Rebecca Sellwood (10) 64
Freya Whyte (9) 65
Claire Anne Holmes (9) 65
Jack Fenna (10) 66
Nabila Jalil (10) 66
April Street (10) 66
Tyler Keith Humphry (10) 67
Phoebe Fulcher (8) 67
Millie Sturgess (9) 67
Leyla Ozgul (9) 68
Cally Summer Webb (8) 68
Kiriana Oliver (9) 68
Audrey Lam (9) 69
Lauryn Garner (10) 69
Holly Tinney (8) 69
Lucy Greenfield (10) 70
Reegan Byrne (8) 70
Bayleigh Wicks (9) 70
Brooke Rennie (10) 71
Jamie Gray (10) 71
Owen Crook (10) 71
Jade Leah Mason (9) 72
Abbie Sketcher (10) 72

Drew Taylor (9)	72
Taya Byrne (10)	73
Marcus Talbot-Roe (9)	73
Anna Townsend (10)	73
Jessica Rose Cornwall (9)	74
Katie Lumb (9)	74
Indigo Amelia Muirhead (10)	74
Georgia Freeman (9)	75
Rhys Rannochan (11)	75
Lisa Chung (10)	75
Sapphire Lewis (9)	76
Stacie Lovell (10)	76
Abigail Harker (9)	76
Hannah Kim Dowse (9)	77
Paige Ballard (9)	77
Ryan Cole (9)	77
Jack Marlow (10)	78
Jade Chappell (10)	78
Henry Tearle (9)	78
Courtney Eagle (10)	79
Luke Heather (10)	79
George Bowers (9)	79

Highfield CE Primary School
Aamir Hamza Rajput (8)	80
Maggie Foster (10)	81
Jimin Yim (9)	82
Ellie Lewis (9)	83
Aimee Rayner (8)	84
Olivia Manger-Webber (8)	85
Raluca Alexii (8)	86
Wozniarski Patryk (9)	87
Chris Lotery (8)	87

Netley Abbey Junior School
Jake Baker (10)	88
Eleanor Serpell-Stevens (11)	89
Abby Parker (10)	90
Katie-Lynn Lucas (10)	90
Matthew Hooper (10)	91
Charlie Felton (11)	91
Ella Purkiss (9)	92
Amber Jones (7)	92

Ellie Nelson (11)	93
Georgia Henry-Dobbyn (7)	93
Jasmine Florence Dyer (9)	94
Megan Victoria Elliott (9)	94
Ella Jane Clark (8)	95
Charlotte Captain (7)	95
Leonie Bath (10)	96
Bethany Battle (10)	96
Isabel Scott (8)	97
Hannah Buckley (9)	97
Hannah Thompson (7)	98
Henry Hammond (8)	98
Heather Robins (11)	99
Matthew Benney (9)	99
Ami Hewlett (10)	100
Amber Parker (8)	100
Alex Ings (10)	101
Anna Rogers (10)	101
Daisy An Smith (8)	102
Elyse Marshall (8)	102
Tomas Shacklady-Suarez (7)	103
Jasmine Charles-Smith (8)	103
Yasmin Paddon (7)	104
Brooke Wilkinson (10)	104
Andrew Pimm (10)	105
Ellie-Mae D'Ambrosio (8)	105
Joseph Cann (7)	106
Gabrielle Thorne (9)	106
Harry Robinson (8)	107
Abigail Hooper (8)	107
William Fox (8)	108
Millie James (7)	108
Chloe Cook (11)	109
Amy Blann (10)	109
Grace Burnard (7)	110
Lilly Hughes (8)	110
Jessica Parslow (7)	111
Sarah Hewlett (7)	111
Lewis Clay (8)	112
Ryan McDonnell (8)	112
Sophie Harker (7)	112
Jason Leach (10)	113
Lewis Gale (7)	113

Nicole Ojeda Leo (10) 113	Georgia King (10) 130
Jack Simmons (10) 114	Amy Hilton 130
Bradley Skelton (8) 114	Grace Halligan (10) 131
Ellie-Mae Smith (8) 114	Billy Beeson (10) 131
Courtney Roberts (11) 115	Jake Spooner (10) 131
Abigail Bowens (7) 115	Jake Pritchard (9) 132
Ellie-Mae Lowbridge (7) 116	Natasha Gibbs 132
Georgia Robinson (10) 116	Amy Thompson 132
Callum Crotty (7) 116	Charlie Weekes 133
Daphne Barge (10) 117	Helena Beachey-Tendyra (9) 133
Kai Burden (7) 117	Charlotte Pugh 133
Molly Moore (7) 117	Tazmin Toms (10) 134
Jake Spanner (7) 118	Sam Morgan (10) 134
Leainya Burden (9) 118	Charlotte Elford (9) 134
Billy Houghton (8) 118	Lucy Moxom (11) 135
Alisha Homer (10) 119	Leah Gill 135
Jacob Smith (11) 119	Lewis Reeves 135
Ellen Mockett (7) 119	Luke Lewis (11) 136
Jay Rowe (7) 120	James Mantle (10) 136
Nathan Gale (8) 120	Daniel Stone 136
Ciara Lewis (8) 120	Oliver Boyland 137
Imogen Beesley (10) 121	Natasha Hall 137
Neil Woodgate (8) 121	Ryan Pope 137
Sam Fields (8) 121	Katie Lenton 138
Jacob Clothier (7) 122	Jamie Ellis (10) 138
Shannon Johnson (7) 122	Lauren Bailey 138
Kayley Carson (7) 122	Kira Marsh 139
Reece Griffiths (8) 123	Issy Cryer 139
Jayden Davies (7) 123	Bethan Keen 139
	Luke Green 140
	Tom Clover (9) 140
	Jos Whitehorn (10) 140
	Ryan Drayton 141

St Luke's CE Primary School, Sway

James Clarke (9) 124
Suzy Judd 124
Jasmine Roberts 125
Racheal Brangan (10) 125
Fraser Owen (11) 126
Robbie Stafford (10) 126
Ryan Jones (10) 127
Maisie Ovenden 127
Samantha Claven 128
Craig Dearnley 128
Lauren Stevens 129
Joseph Lewis (10) 129

St Swithun's Primary School, Portsmouth

Daniel Chapero-Hall (10) 141
Isabel Thompson-Whiteside (9) 142
Aleksandra Ruzik (9) 143
Helena Cox-Smith (10) 144
Francesca Furtado Mills (10) 144
India Beaumont (10) 145
Gaia Osborne (9) 145
Freya Temple (10) 146

Sophie Carabott (9) 146
Patrick Carden (9) 147

Stoke Park Junior School
Daniel Coleman (10) 147
Tyler Kowalewicz (10) 148
Lucy Spake (10) 148
Maddie Lewis (10) 149
Kieran Sheppard-Laing (10) 149
Joshua Moore (9) 150
Jack Ryves (10) 150
Max Pitman (11) 151
Jasmine Sims (10) 151
Oliver Wright (7) 152
Louie Meleder (9) 152
Tasmin Smith (9) 152
Ben Sutcliffe (9) 153
Simon Hancock (9) 153
Elizabeth Earl (9) 153
Lewis Pople (10) 154
Jack Lawrence (10) 154
Alice Wilmot (9) 154
Ben Vincent (10) 155
James Beadle (9) 155
Daniel Whitehead (10) 155
Jamie Cattle (10) 156
Samantha Williams (10) 156
Thomas Moorcroft (10) 156
Mitchell Shilling (10) 157
Shea Manning (9) 157
Connor Gregory (10) 157
Joshua Gissing (9) 158
Jordon Hatton (10) 158
Daisy Jones (10) 158
Emma Kane (9) 159
Callum Ward (9) 159
Hayden Doust (9) 159
Samuel Gray (10) 160
Deanne Sara Smith (9) 160
Lucas Bright (9) 160
Elena Beckett-Oxenham (9) 161
Callan Winstanley (9) 161
Sally Waite (9) 161

Luke Spring (9) 162
Jake Haysom (9) 162
Jack Bird (9) 162

Tresnant Junior School
Hayley Winstanley (10) 163
Bradley Luke Rance (9) 164
Kyisha Hansler (9) 164
Meg Skinner (10) 165
Tyler Allen (9) 165
Natasha Richardson (10) 166
Lennox Ryan Moore (11) 166
Kate Pearce (10) 167
Liberty Gordon (10) 167
Grace Shepherd (10) 168
Arron Peter Gooderham (11) 168
Caitlin Hunter (11) 169
Brandon Moore (11) 169
Owen Larkin (10) 170
Kira Bravington (9) 170
Curtis Tait (9) 170

The Poems

Kidnapped

My body was shoved into a tiny sack,
Frost grew round my eyelashes.
In a flash, I was on a narrow bus
And the breeze flew through my ears.
A cold shiver ran down my thin spine.
I felt water pouring outside,
Like God was shedding tears.
I felt my heart disintegrate into millions of pieces.
My teeth chattered together as I trembled with fear.
Everyone stared at me, eye to eye,
Wondering why I was crying.
Warm tears trickled down my dry cheeks,
As I experienced the saddest thing ever . . .
Kidnap.

Ashton Crosby (10)
Beechwood Junior School

A Ghostly Hunt!

Dark, gloomy, scary, cold
I hope this ghost is very old

Creeping quietly through the house
I hear a noise but it's only a mouse

Looking out for ghostly figures
Ooh it's very cold, it gives me the shivers

On the stairs I see a figure getting closer, getting bigger
Is this what I've come to see?
Well that's between you and me.

Lauren Grant (9)
Beechwood Junior School

The War

The never-ending catastrophic war,
People wish to introduce some kind of law.
Fearful sobs cry, 'Will they come back?'
With hope that their relatives are not under attack.
As the trigger of the gun starts to crack,
The soldiers then know there is no way back.
Then ceremonies and funerals are arranged,
And families and friends cry in pain.
Why couldn't the clock go back,
To a time when there wasn't the *war!*

Hannah Olivia Price (10)
Beechwood Junior School

My Pet Guinea Pig

My guinea pig can hop, jump and fly,
My guinea pig can say hello and goodbye,
He likes to eat apples and grapes,
And because he's a superhero,
He wears colourful capes.

I definitely love him more than most,
And as I say this he would start to boast,
'Although I am sometimes quite a pest,
My owner still thinks I'm the very best.'

Sophie Stirrat (9)
Beechwood Junior School

Dolphins

Dolphins are magic, they live in the sea,
When I go swimming they come close to me.
Instead of talking, they make a squeak,
Then I feel happy and start to speak.

Their skins are smooth, slippery and grey,
They love to jump, dive and play.
They have hours of fun with lots to do,
Maybe one day they will play with you.

Shani Lambert (7)
Beechwood Junior School

Fairies

Fairies, fairies all around
as I sit they're everywhere.
With delicate wings and tiny smiles
that glitter in the moonlight.
If you dare to sit and wait,
they will come to you tonight.

Kayleigh Barnes (7)
Beechwood Junior School

My Name Is Hollie

Hello, my name is Hollie.
I have a friend called Polly.
I also have a wee, sweet dolly named Molly.
When Molly goes shopping
She takes a brolly and a trolley.
What a wally, Molly.

Hollie Chapman (9)
Beechwood Junior School

The Pet Shop

'A tabby cat wearing a hat?'
'No, just some cat food please.'
'What about a dog or a Japanese frog?'
'No, just some cat food please.'
'Would you like a fish but not for a dish?'
'No, just some cat food please.'
'How about a mouse to keep in your house?'
'No, just some cat food please.'
'What about a lizard but don't lose it in a blizzard?'
'No, just some cat food please.'
'What about a rabbit with a terrible habit?'
'No, just some cat food please.'
'What about a parrot eating a carrot?'
'No, just some cat food please.'
'What about a bird or a rhino herd?'
'No, just some cat food please.'
'How about a monkey who is very, very hunky?'
'Are you deaf? No, just some cat food please!'
'Sorry dear, I couldn't hear.'
'Just some cat food please.'
'Oh yes, it's right over here.'

Charlotte Remnant (10)
Bosmere Junior School

Autumn

The tree looks down at the sparkling frosty floor,
Covered in leaves,
Dancing and prancing in the wind.

The trees are swooshing in the howling wind,
While the wind is whistling at the prancing golden leaves.

The golden leaves falling mysteriously,
Again and again on the sparkly ground,
While the brown conkers laugh.

Skye Palmer (10)
Bosmere Junior School

At The Corner Shop

'Crisps or toffee, paper cup of coffee?'
'No just some sherbet please.'
'Roses are red, violets are blue.'
'No, just some sherbet please.'
'Gobstopper big or liquorice twist?'
'No, just some sherbet please.'
'A chocolate bar or gummy bear jar?'
'No, just some sherbet please.'
'A cold ice lolly or a book called Jolly?'
'No, just some sherbet please.'
'Edible beads or bouncy bees?'
'No, just some sherbet please.'
'Boo boo dummies or order some curry?'
'Don't you understand, just some sherbet please!'
'Oh why didn't you say, we're very busy today.'
'OK, thank you, I'll be going now.'
'We also sell . . . '
'Argh!'

Georgie Donnelly (10)
Bosmere Junior School

At The Pet Shop

'Gerbil or bird, is that your third?'
'No, just a fish please.'
'Budgie or snake, or one that's fake?'
'No, just a fish please.'
'A bunny that's funny?'
'No, just a fish please.'
'Fox or pig, or one that's big?'
'No, just a fish please.'
'Squirrel or ox, or another fox?'
'Oh for goodness' sake, just give me a fish please!'
'Certainly madam, coming right up, goldfish or haddock?'
'Forget it, nothing's worth this!'

Darcy Matthews (11)
Bosmere Junior School

Autumn Poem

Yellow and brown crinkling leaves
calmly floating through the fresh open air.
The trees sway in the wind like a Spanish dancer
stomping in the moonlight.

Spectacular fireworks happily shooting
through the dull sky making a crystal.
Smelling the awful stench of the burning bonfires
in the sooty dark night.

Squirrels scuttling joyfully around carefully collecting their
magnificent nuts ready for hibernation in the frosty cold winter.
Hedgehogs are building nests as they realise winter is near.

The black dark night spookily draws in
as the exquisite daylight fades away.
Warm summer days draw to a close
as the bitter winter draws in.

Chloe Bradbury (10)
Bosmere Junior School

Spring's Beauty

Spring has a beauty
A beauty indeed
It lays out its flowers
With precision and care
And wonders which creatures will lie beneath there

It could be the bumblebee or the woodlouse
It could be the beetle or a small field mouse

It could be a spider, its food to come soon
It could be a caterpillar making a cocoon

So many things could lie beneath
The floral decoration
Provided by spring.

Rebecca Simes (10)
Bosmere Junior School

Autumn

The trees loomed over me,
And looked at me with disdain,
As one day their friends will fall,
And will never see them again.
The fireworks were attached to the black velvet sky,
They whizz and pop like champagne,
They sparkle as if telling a story,
And shimmer again and again.
The leaves crunched like biscuits,
They yelped as if they were hurt,
They danced around in the howling wind,
And brushed around in the dirt.
I run around in the playgrounds,
Almost every day,
I listen out for lovely sounds,
I wish the weather was like this in May!

Rebekah Wells (11)
Bosmere Junior School

Autumn

Leaves gently dancing on the ground,
Trees slowly turning bare,
Leaves quietly whispering to each other,
Trees standing very lonely,
With no green leaves there.

Fireworks bursting into flames,
Astonished people stare at the sight,
The fireworks are a huge scream,
From a little girl at Hallowe'en who has had a fright.

Pumpkins and ripe plums,
Everybody collecting food,
The harvest is a big parade, having fun,
Everyone in a good mood.

Erin Offord (10)
Bosmere Junior School

Autumn Poem

The heavy rain is crystal-clear like water from a tap.
The squirrels are busy hunting ready for a cold and frosty winter.
The crunchy leaves are as bronzed as a polished penny
tumbling across the floor.
Can you hear the bare branches swaying in the howling wind?
Have you seen the autumn sky and the fluffy clouds that overtake it?
What about the autumn breeze rushing past your face?
Have you smelt the smoke from the burning bonfires
in the neighbour's garden?
Have you seen the fireworks in the starry sky?

Autumn is a time for you to wrap up cosy and warm.
Autumn is a time for you to sit by the fire.
Autumn is a time for you to drink warm drinks before you go to bed.
Autumn is a time for you to enjoy what it has to offer.

Sasha Harris (10)
Bosmere Junior School

Autumn

Early in the evening when all is cool and crisp,
We wait by the fire, long shiny days.

The summer ends and days get shorter,
The bronzed leaves are falling, this is autumn, a lovely time.
When all of nature has come to shine.

The squirrels run around in the trees looking for sticks
And the remaining green leaves.
The badgers and moles look up at the sky to see
The changing colours over time.

On weekend days, when we're out to play,
The wind blows strong and the large trees sway,
The time has come, this is autumn.

Toby Andrew Morton (10)
Bosmere Junior School

Autumn

The trees waved at me with happiness,
They were tall walls looming over me.
The leaves were dancing with loneliness,
As they fell onto my knee.

The fireworks were like disco balls,
Being thrown into the velvet night sky.
The bonfires were flaming hot waterfalls,
Coloured by red dye.

Golden corn being cut into shreds,
The apples being chopped,
Like the wood from many sheds,
The seasons will never stop.

Rebecca Ede-Jones (10)
Bosmere Junior School

Autumn

The trees were swishing and waving,
Leaves slowly twirling down on the ground.
The leaves danced and pranced on the frosty ground,
Like a graceful ballerina.

The fireworks were like galloping jewels,
Screams echoing from all around,
Laughing and rattling sweets was the only sound.
The moon was like a bowl of ice cream floating in the midnight sky.

The golden corn waving in the wind,
The apples jumping branch to branch.

Sharna Capel-Watson (10)
Bosmere Junior School

Autumn

The trees of autumn lose all their leaves,
The trees of autumn waved at me
as I ran past collecting conkers,
The sound of me walking through the crisp crunching leaves,
The smooth feeling of conkers
that have freshly fallen off their homes.

The fireworks filled the night sky like one hundred stars,
The smell of the thick black smoke from the crackling fire,
The fireworks screamed as children run around,
Sparklers glow all around like the sun on a hot summer's day.

Rebecca Meades (10)
Bosmere Junior School

Horse And Ponies Show

I can smell the disgusting horse manure
I can smell the beautiful horses' coats
I can smell the fresh air breezing in my face.

I can hear the people chatting
As loud as an elephant can stomp her feet
I can hear the horses' hooves clattering as loud as a bell
I can hear the ponies neigh in my light pale face.

I can taste the delicious ice creams - strawberry!
I can taste the fur in my delicate sensitive mouth
I can taste the mouth-watering chilli that was sold.

I can feel the horses blowing my face as fast as a cheetah
I can touch the horse in my hand which is as soft as a teddy bear
I can touch the beautiful, tall, different-coloured horses
In the palm of my hand.

I can see the horses jumping as high as a giraffe's neck
I can see the horse's mane shine in my face
I can see the wonderful horses and ponies.

Kaitlan-Pfeiffer-Richardson (9)
Corpus Christi Primary School

The Big Battle

Before:

The silence is deafening
No movement
All I see is nothingness
An empty war ground
The armour I wear is clutching me
As if it's not wanting to let go
I taste the armour's metal
Cold and bitter in my mouth.

During:

I see the cannons blowing away
I hear a terrifying scream
Then I notice my friend has gone
From my side forever
I smell the smoke as it overtakes my nose
Strangling me
And I want to run
The taste of blood runs down my face
Or is it tears?

After:

I see my side cheering
Victory is in the air
I sit, hearing my heart beat
Overtaking my senses
The smell of smoke
Surrounding my face
Choking me
I still have the metallic taste in my mouth
Tears drop from my eyes
Is this really victory?

Charis Almond (9)
Corpus Christi Primary School

Church Is Beautiful

Church can be boring
The Latin words are endless
Yes, it's beautiful!

The choir is like angel voices
You see them singing most of the mass
They hold up the church with their voices as pillars
Isn't it beautiful?

The tingle of the bells are healing
They're like saints whispering
Their distant voices echo, 'Amen, amen'
Isn't it beautiful?

The sweet scent of burning incense
Fills your whole body with joy
It's a smell that changes horrid emotions
Isn't it beautiful?

The giving of bread at communion
Is like a tablet guaranteed for kindness
Medicine designed for a living soul
Isn't it beautiful?

As we shake hands with each other
A peculiar feeling builds up inside me
Everything in church becomes enjoyable
Everything seems beautiful!

Rebecca Galbraith (9)
Corpus Christi Primary School

I Feel Clothes

I feel good,
I touch the softness grabbing my body,
The warmth of the red wool keeps me happy and contented,
I feel good.

I feel lonely,
I can see the pockets to put my hands in,
I see the spare strands pulling me in and in,
I feel lonely.

I feel tempted,
I taste the spilt ketchup all down the tickly strands of my scarf,
I will get tangled,
I feel tempted.

I feel excited,
I hear the washing machine going round and round and round,
I feel excited.

I feel like a flower,
I smell the washing powder taking over my lungs,
The smell is so romantic,
I feel like a flower.

Lydia Weedon (9)
Corpus Christi Primary School

The Sea

Walking along the sandy beach,
I saw the sun setting behind the crashing waves
Punching the jetty, bruising its legs
The scaly fish jumping out of the water
Whispering unidentified songs.

I could smell the salty, coral, blue sea
And the fish being chased by the giant blue monster
Its teeth like fingers, clutching them in.

I could feel the golden sand between my toes
As I took off my sandals
The sand scorching my feet, sending warmth up my body.

I could taste the fish and chips as we sat down to eat
Comforting and sour all at once.

The waves, I could hear them as they smashed
And crashed on the shore
Angry or playful, no one could tell
The sea, the sea, the sea.

Olivia Powell (9)
Corpus Christi Primary School

Air Balloon

I can see the air balloon rising like the sun
I can see the colourful balloon burning like a barbecue
I can see the red flickering gas burning up.

I can touch the hot air balloon heating up
I can touch the heavy sand bag, heavy as a knight's armour
I can touch the wood cast hitting the floor.

I can smell the smoke burning in the air
I can smell the rubber flowing everywhere
I can smell the trees blossoming in the air.

I can taste the hot dog van on the ground.

Taylor Shawyer
Corpus Christi Primary School

Where Am I?

I hear the cry of the ghosts surrounding me
I hear the giggles from the witches
I hear the squeak and an eek from the bats
Singing their terrifying song.

I taste the magic gushing down my throat
I taste the dust from the cobwebs
I taste the sweat that falls from my head.

I see green warts printed on the witches' faces
I see the rats scampering across the room
I see the frightening spider drinking flies' gruesome blood.

I feel my hand as it shakes and trembles with fear
I feel cobwebs as they brush against my arm
I feel the puddles of blood as I walk closer to the witches.

I smell the dust as it tickles my nose
I smell the witches' potion as they stir and pour
I smell the group of witches walk towards me.

Maddison Ferguson (9)
Corpus Christi Primary School

A Fairy Wonderland

See - I see the fairies fluttering, collecting soft yellow pollen
to make their lives richer.

Hear - I hear the shining fairies singing through the trees,
making every note as sweet as a singing blue bird.

Touch - I touch the tiny toadstool sitting in the grass,
I feel like an intruder invading.

Taste - I taste the fairy tea fluttering down my throat,
as we sit in the grass.

Smell - I smell the sweet fairy flowers flowing up my nose.

Rachael Butler (9)
Corpus Christi Primary School

The Black And White Horse

Galloping through the meadows
A black and white horse
I can taste the fear surrounding
As the human approaches

I can touch the black tail
As the horse runs with nerves

I can hear him breathing hard
As I walk forwards, a snap of twig unnerves him

I can smell the wildness engulfing my nose
Trapping my other senses

I can see his shimmering mane
The horse's amazing coat
As I begin to get closer.

Elise Sherwin (9)
Corpus Christi Primary School

The Dream Of Witches

I touch the unidentified lurking in the night
Their arms wrapping round me
Piercing with their petrifying eyes
Like daggers through my heart.

I taste claws clinging hold of my neck
Tearing, ripping
I taste the blood, its metallic edge cuts me.

I see the unidentified
The horrid eyes like seaweed glowing in the murky water
The sound is terrifying.

Black clouds engulf me, sweep me away
The witches, they have come back
It is a nightmare.

Natty Haywood (9)
Corpus Christi Primary School

Watching War In The Wind

In war I hear souls scream,
but nobody hears,
shots are pushed out of the guns.

In war I feel coldness and raindrops,
I feel dust of the tank choking my lungs,
shaking the ground, beneath my feet.

In war I taste the smoke from the bombs,
I taste metallic liquid from people dying,
I taste violence.

In war I see people fall and soldiers run and charge,
fear in their eyes
I smell smoke rushing up my nose, its fingers clinging to my throat,
the sense of heroes floating in the wind.

Ben Bramley
Corpus Christi Primary School

Poppies

Poppies represent peace
They symbolise blood from the battlefield
As the moon goes up and the sun goes down
The poppies grow
Symbolising the lives that once were.

I see poppies scattered on the field
The sound is silent, empty, it's like no one is there.

Everything is so soft like a giant cloud floating on a dream
I taste the fresh open air
My mouth is fresh, my tongue is fresh
I smell the dirt blowing, blocking my lungs
And holding my sense.

War is a nightmare.

Ollie Conaghan (9)
Corpus Christi Primary School

Farm

I see the animals chasing the birds and also going wild and loony
and the farmer feeding the horses and milking the cows.

I see funny animals gather around the fresh green grass
ready to go and start to be cleaned by the farmer in the stables.

I hear the animals like the cows and horses neighing and mooing
waiting for the farmer to come along.

I taste the fresh soft breeze slowly sway side to side and just pass
my face very fast, as fast as a sports car
can race a rabbit to the finish line.

I smell the fleas on the cows and horses and the old hay
and mud on the dirty, muddy field.

I touch the rabbits as they slowly hop all over the show and go hyper.

Leah Cox (10)
Corpus Christi Primary School

Space Adventure

I see the space rocket power, it's as low as a twig
As I fly past the dark side of the moon
I see that it is as dark as the night sky
The stars look so bright like a lamp in the dark room.

My space outfit feels as tough as a rock
As I walk on the moon, I touch a moon rock,
It is as smooth as a ball
I touch the controls, it makes me feel like a shooting star.

I get back on the space rocket and taste some of my space food
It is as tasty as a fish sandwich
I go outside to get some space rock
I taste some of the space air, it is like nothing
As I land on the Earth, I taste victory, it is as sweet as a sand cone.

Dylan Bridle (9)
Corpus Christi Primary School

In The Park

Children are running like wild animals
playing around while shouting and roaring.

Soft fresh green grass gathers between my fingers,
while I breathe the fresh cool air.

A bit of chewy ham and cheese sandwich
from the picnic basket slowly slides down my throat
with a taste which lasts a minute or two.

Feeling a fruit of gold, then bite a mouthful,
feels full with flavour.

Vicious dogs are coming, I can hear them,
I can smell them and I can see them,
I hope the dogs won't go near me.

Angela De La Fuente (9)
Corpus Christi Primary School

The Sea

I can see the blue water making waves as fast as a cheetah
See the dark blue shiny whale like a glass.

Hear the shimmering waves rushing up and down
Hear the splash of people going into the water to swim.

Smell the fresh salty air which is like Walkers crisps
You can smell the food that people brought.

I can touch the green slippery soft seaweed
Which is like green grass.

You can taste the salty water which is cold, freezing and shivering
Also it is a taste of real salt
You can taste the food that you brought to the sea
Which might taste crunchy.

Liya Shaji (9)
Corpus Christi Primary School

My Pets And Me

I see their beautiful faces, their eyes smiling at me
Like glistening balls of sunlight every morning
Their touch comforting my heart like a blanket.

I taste the love as I kiss my little cat Elsa
Breathing over my face at night protecting, caring.

I hear my little rabbit's tiny claws scurrying
Around her spacious hutch
The sweet noise consoles any loneliness.

I feel the smooth downy fur at night
And in the morning its sensations pour up my arm.

The fishy breath of my cat reminds me of the trips to the sea
My cat and my rabbit, two small parts of me.

Laura Smith (9)
Corpus Christi Primary School

The Sea

The blue waves splicing side to side
With the soft rocky seaweed and the fishy disgusting smell
As you get off the rocky slippery sea.

You walk along and you take a little bite of your crunchy sandwich
And the sand slips between your fingers.

And when you sit on the rocky sand you hear the waves
Slipping side to side as fast as a cheetah.

Then in the corner of your eye you see a whale
And it makes a splash as huge as elephants' feet
Then you find sand with no rocks in
You sit down and you see a whale
You are astonished.

Rachel Preston (9)
Corpus Christi Primary School

Church

I smell the candles burning and the incense spreading
round the room engulfing every part.

I feel God's love touching my heart
and the glory bringing me light.

I hear the gospels from the Bible
with the messages helping me to understand more.

I taste the bread and wine with the Holy Spirit guiding me.

I look down into my heart and see Jesus helping the love
of people and the kindness of the world.

Leah Clements (9)
Corpus Christi Primary School

Untitled

You see the crystal blue water sliding through your hands
As fast as a greyhound running round a track.
See sparkly multicoloured fish looking for food to eat.
Hear the fish jumping out of the water.
You can hear the wind whistling through my hair.
I can touch the bright green leather seat that I am sitting on.
I touch the soft brown sand when I get back to shore.
I taste the salted water that tastes saltier than ready salted crisps.
You can feel the wind pulling you away from the comfy seats.
The fish feel so slimy that it is slimier than some bouncy putty.

Ethan Barker
Corpus Christi Primary School

Wizards And Witches

Wizard and witch making a brew,
With eyeballs, frogs' legs and kangaroo.
Chanting the words for a spell,
Hoping everything would go well.

The cauldron bubbled, hissed and spat,
This scared the witch's black cat.
Smoke raised from the castle's floor,
Then came a knock from the front door.

'Trick or treat!' the children cried,
The wizard and witch were horrified.
Then the wizard encouraged them in,
Taking notice that they were thin.

Giving them sweets to fatten them so,
Not long now till the start of the show.
They fed them the potion as a drink,
The children then began to shrink.

The wizard gave the children an antidote,
When the witch found out she tried to cut his throat.
The wizard was just a little too quick,
And gave her an almighty kick.

Disarming the witch with a flick of his wand,
She then found herself standing in a deep pond.
As she couldn't swim she began to drown,
The wizard had finally got rid of his frown.

It was midnight and getting late,
The children said, 'Goodbye,' at the old rusty gate.
The wizard then decided not to be mean,
But you never know until next Hallowe'en.

Megan Bourne (10)
Elson Junior School

Friendship

Try to play games, so anyone can join the fun.
Give it a try, everyone.
Friendship is the care for everyone.
Here's a story, everyone,
The story is a fairy tale
Hello, can you play?
Sorry I can't!
Can I come?
OK everyone.
They came to the park.
Can you play?
Sorry I can't!
I want to have a run in the sun.
Can I come?
OK everyone.
They went to the skateboard ramp.
Hello, can you play?
Sorry, I can't!
I want to have a run in the sun.
Can I come?
OK everyone.
Then they got to the sun.
Run, run, run everyone in the sun.
Can we paint a picture in school?
OK, what a lovely picture you have got.

Emma Charleston (8)
Elson Junior School

Pony Show Me

Pony show me how to fly
So I can reach to the sky
Up and down all around
It will be so fun!

Emma Cains (9)
Elson Junior School

Christmas Countdown

24, 23, 22, 21
Christmas is the time
To have lots of fun
20, 19, 18, 17
I love all the
Decorations
Red, silver and green
16, 15, 14, 13
Father Christmas is
Very unseen
12, 11, 10, 9
All the stars in the
Sky shine
8, 7, 6, 5
All the music makes
Me dance and jive
4, 3, 2, 1
The countdown is
Down at last, at last!

Emily Chandler (10)
Elson Junior School

Dolphin, Dolphin

Dolphin, dolphin
Swimming everywhere
In the water and in the air,
Dolphin, dolphin
Squirming for some fish
When I leave them I begin to miss,
Dolphin, dolphin
I love them to bits,
I love to see them flit,
Dolphin, dolphin,
They're the best!

Annasley Sheen (9)
Elson Junior School

Dobby The Frog

Dobby the frog had a bob
And her hair is golden ginger
Her hair is like cotton
Right down to her bottom
She likes Hannah Montana
And she has a banner
You may think she's like Harry Potter
But she's more like Barry Trotter
Her eyes are blue
That is how she joins the pirate crew
Her mouth is big
She has a pet pig
She had a lot past
On the ship she put up the masts
It was a roller coaster ride
Before she lied
She can play the drum
But then her lips go numb
What a hard life Dobby the frog has.

Hazel Camburn (8)
Elson Junior School

Hallowe'en, Hallowe'en

H allowe'en is nearly here,
A witch, a cat, a broom,
L oving all the pranks we do,
L aughing down the streets,
O h we love our sweets,
W e can dress how we like,
E veryone's having sweets,
E veryone had a great night,
N ow Hallowe'en is in the past.

Christmas is coming fast.

Kelsey Barnes (9)
Elson Junior School

Animal Similes

Gallop like a horse
Fly like a bird
Sprint across a field
Like a sheep in a herd.

Rush like a cheetah
Leap like a cat
Fly through the night sky
Like a black mysterious bat.

Race like a tiger
Jump like a frog
Roll in a puddle
Like a pig in a bog.

Dash like a cheetah
Float like a fish
Swim in the sea
Like a fish in a dish.

Chelsi Reed (8)
Elson Junior School

Sweets

Big sweets, small sweets
Blue sweets, pink sweets
Yummy sweets, horrible sweets
Exciting sweets, boring sweets
Popping sweets, normal sweets
Baby sweets, adult sweets
My sweets, their sweets
20 sweets, 10 sweets
Strawberry sweets, raspberry sweets
Bagged sweets, packet sweets
Shop sweets, Charlie and the Chocolate Factory sweets
Chocolate river, toffee sweets.

Ellodie Beale (9)
Elson Junior School

Me And My Friend

I went to the cinema
With my friend Heather
'Cause it wasn't nice weather
So we got tea together
It was pouring now
And we bought an umbrella
That's what I did with
My friend Heather!

I went to the park
With my friend Heather
'Cause it was nice weather
So we played together
It was sunny now
And we bought an ice cream
That's what I did with
My friend Heather!

Rhiannon Smith (9)
Elson Junior School

Creepy-Crawlies

Creepy-crawlies
Give me the ghoulies,
In your hair,
Everywhere.
In your eyes hope you don't get sties,
Maybe they should make a potion,
Wipe them all out,
Put them in a different nation.
In your ear, up your nose,
Even up and down your clothes.
Get rid of them I'm telling you now,
It will make the Queen bow.
So get rid of them now!

Eden Heath (9)
Elson Junior School

Chocolate

Chocolate, chocolate, rich or sweet,
Chocolate, chocolate, what a treat!
Chocolate, chocolate, rich or poor,
Chocolate, chocolate, give me some more.
Chocolate, chocolate, white or black,
Chocolate, chocolate, it's not a bit of tack!
Chocolate, chocolate, love or hate,
Chocolate, chocolate, but please offer it to your mate.
Chocolate, chocolate, cold or hot,
Chocolate, chocolate, you can melt it in a pot.
Chocolate, chocolate, stop and stare,
Chocolate, chocolate everywhere.
Chocolate, a whole world full of it!

Taylor Campion (9)
Elson Junior School

It's Time To Read!

It's time to read,
Come on!
I'll take the lead,
So get a book and take a look.
Don't be afraid,
Read the book you've made.
So turn the page,
But try not to make the letters fade.
So dig in or . . .
I'll chuck you into the book!

Jade Sheppard (10)
Elson Junior School

Slippers

Red slippers, blue slippers,
Fluffy slippers, princess slippers,
Cool slippers, funny bunny slippers,
Cake slippers, puffy slippers,
Cool slippers, small slippers,
Big slippers, teachers' slippers,
Baby slippers, kids' slippers,
Christmas slippers, Hallowe'en slippers,
Slippers, slippers, slippers, slippers.

Leah Robinson (9)
Elson Junior School

The Ocean

The ocean.
The ocean tumbles.
The angry, rough ocean tumbles.
The angry, rough ocean tumbles fiercely.
The angry, rough ocean tumbles fiercely
next to the sandy, calm beach.
In the dark, gloomy night, the angry, rough ocean tumbles fiercely
next to the sandy, calm beach.
I feel excited.

Rachel Tapp (7)
Elson Junior School

The Sparkly Sea

I can see rapid waves splashing in the middle of the rock pool.
I can hear children laughing noisily in the sea.
I can feel sand slipping through my fingers.
I can smell hot dogs cooking in a van.
I can taste ice cream melting in my mouth.
I like the beach.

Erin Tanner (8)
Elson Junior School

Shoes, Shoes, Shoes

Big shoes
Little shoes, red shoes, blue shoes
Pink shoes, yellow shoes
Old shoes, new shoes
School shoes, cool shoes
Fancy shoes, baby shoes
Flat shoes, small shoes
Horse shoes, more shoes.

Thea Hogg (9)
Elson Junior School

The Sea

The sea
The sea is shimmering
The sparkly sea is shimmering
The sparkly sea is shimmering sadly
The sparkly sea is shimmering sadly on the moonlit beach
The sparkly sea is shimmering sadly on the moonlit beach in the middle of the night
I say I'll be his friend.

Alegria Tracey (7)
Elson Junior School

We Are All Unique

Do you know, do you now why, why everyone is different
and even when they die?
Why did God do it, to every single one, why did God do it,
why, oh why, oh why?
I wish He could tell me but He's really hard to find,
has anybody seen Him? Oh I really wish you had.
Do you know, do you know why, why everyone's different
and even when they die?

Millie Murtagh (9)
Elson Junior School

The Beach

I can see cute baby seashells spreading along the sandy beach.
I can hear fast waves bobbing along the rocks.
I can feel smooth sand kissing my whole body.
I can smell salty sea sniffing my nose.
I can taste salty sea washing my mouth.
I feel cheerful at the beach.

Alefiya Khedapa (7)
Elson Junior School

Wonder

Wonder is like a glimpse of gold
The colour of orange sparks spitting from a fire
The red on a rose petal
All these colours are hidden in wonder
Wonder is like drops of water drip dropping from a loose tap
It sounds like owls chorusing at the strike of midnight
Wonder is like the fresh mint Aero
It's the delicate smell of chlorine fresh from a pool
Wonder looks like a lonely tree rustling its leaves in the field
It looks like a churchyard full of graves
Some old and crumbling
Some new and smooth
Wonder feels like a bubbling sort of feeling
It feels like that shiver or sensation
When you win a race
Wonder reminds me of seeing my twin brother and my big brother
Jumping off a big rock
And when they landed all the fish separated within a second
Wonder tastes like a sweet lemon
But with a powerful tang of sourness to it
Wonder can be anything you want it to be
It can even be flabbergasting.

Matilda Everard (10)
Forres Sandle Manor School

Delight

Delight is all colours of the rainbow:
Red, orange, yellow, green, blue, indigo and violet.

Delight has a smell of freshly baked cake:
Yum-yum.

Delight has a sound of laughter
Happy, joyful laughter
Joyful music
With a touch of bounce and spring to it.

Delight has a sight of coloured balloons
People smiling
Having fun
Happy, springy time.

Delight has a touch of soft, comfortable happiness,
A fizz of surprise
And the cool breeze of movement.

Delight has a taste of your favourite food
Perhaps newly buttered toast on your tongue
Or chocolate cake melting in your mouth.

Delight reminds you of . . . what?
A warm, comfortable bed?
A fast moving dance party?
Or just comin' home at the weekend?

Delight is a wonderful feeling of colour, sound, smell and taste.
So if you want to feel it, go and experience it.

Rosie Landon (10)
Forres Sandle Manor School

Fear

The blackness,
The silence of fear, like a raging fire,
That cannot be seen nor heard.
The scared feeling of death, heading your way,
Silently,
A living nightmare.
Fear is phobia,
Fear is the dark forest of no-man's-land,
Fresh poison it may taste of.
Fear is like a shiver down your spine, a warning,
The sound of fading cries is fear.
Smelling of nothing.
You feel like you are being taken over
By something,
Something you can't really see,
Like a pair of yellow eyes in a low dark cloud.
Dark green,
Strange black light.
Fear is like terror,
But almost never-ending.
Fear is fear,
Fear is strange.
Fear can be imaginative,
But it depends on the way you think of it.
The blackness, the silence of fear.

Freddie Skeates (10)
Forres Sandle Manor School

Courage

Electric green, blue so bold,
Neon pink, stand out gold.
Red, warm and bright,
Orange, comforting, holding you tight.
Wrapped up in parents' arms.
Someone's hair when they lift you high
And spin you round and round.
Echoes booming,
Yet not feeling afraid.
War alarms not even stirring you.
Sleeping in a pitch-black room.
The taste of victory, hot and spicy,
But like an ice lolly, fruity cool.
A shimmer, light ahead,
Walking home on a crisp winter's day.
Helping someone; crossing danger,
Riding a roller coaster without holding tight,
Running down a hill with a star speckled sky,
Falling from high, but landing safely,
Trekking a long way home.

Alice Risebrow (10)
Forres Sandle Manor School

Thirst

My mouth was watering
Like a waterfall in the Pacific Islands
It was cold and dry
Like someone had just pumped air down my throat
It felt like I had a small desert inside
It reminds me of when the bath is full of warm soothing water
That keeps you warm
And you pull the plug, all the heat goes
And you get cold.

Joe Cox (11)
Forres Sandle Manor School

Calm

Calm is
when the warming smell of horse breath
is sneaking into my face.
Calm is
when a purple, velvety colour is coming into my mind
making everything go quiet.
Calm is
when the sound of hoof beats is thudding around me
the echo of a neigh entering my ear.
Calm is
when I get a taste of candyfloss popping in my mouth
and fizzing on my tongue.
Calm is
when I see a horse grazing in his field
and every now and then he lifts his head to check
there are no dangers near
Calm is
when I remember my first ride on the beach
and I galloped in the sea.

Georgia Downes (11)
Forres Sandle Manor School

Untitled

The smell of cooking makes me feel hungry.
The smell of the sea makes me remember the fun days
playing on the beach.
The smell of a fire makes me think of Christmas,
sitting with all the wrapping.
The smell of ink makes me think of long, hard days
having an exam.
The smell of petrol makes me think of the pollution
that cities make.
But best of all, the smell of bacon frying
makes me think of my house!

Teddie Pressland (10)
Forres Sandle Manor School

Anger

Anger looks like the darkest of reds,
Like the bubbling lava of a huge volcano.
It has a definite smell of toast,
Burning in a toaster
And no one comes to get it,
It just sits there burning.
The sounds is of fireworks
Banging and sizzling
In the dark, dark sky of the night.
It looks like fireworks too,
Swirling,
Going up and up into the night sky.
It feels like somebody stabbing the sharp end
Of a gleaming knife into my heart.
It reminds me of all the bad and wrong
I have done in my life.
It tastes just like poison and blood in your mouth
Swirling around like a current of water.

Rupert Talfourd-Cook (10)
Forres Sandle Manor School

Happiness

Happiness is a golden yellow
Like the shining sun
It feels soft and comforting
Like a baby puppy
It tastes like fairground candyfloss
Melting in your mouth
It smells of sweet honeysuckle
On a hot summer's day
It reminds me of my family
And holidays in the sun
Happiness is beautiful
Happiness is fun.

Laurie Smith (10)
Forres Sandle Manor School

Excitement

Excitement reminds you of Christmas;
The warm house smelling of mince pies and pinecones,
The bright lights filling the Christmas tree,
You can't help but smile.
Excitement is never dull;
It's yellows, pinks, oranges and reds,
It feels like going to sleep on Christmas Eve,
Knowing that empty stocking will be bursting with presents -
Teddies and my favourite candy canes -
In the morning.
Excitement smells of Christmas pudding steaming on the stove,
It's opening your biggest present on Christmas morning,
Bursting to see what's inside.
Excitement sounds of the rustling and ripping of wrapping paper,
It's getting on my best dress and doing up my hair,
Ready to show my family and friends,
It looks like the sparkling tinsel,
High on the Christmas tree.

Olivia Peters
Forres Sandle Manor School

War

War is the colour of a flash that streaks past you.
War smells like the roses your wife gives you
And of your best friend's body lying limp.
It sounds like the cheer of the crowd
And the bullets and explosions flying past you.
War tastes like the rations they give you
And the blood throbbing out as you are shot.
It looks like the flowers
In the French streets of Le Somme.
War feels like a tingle in your fingers
And the blood of so many people is on your hands
War reminds me of the lost and fallen on all sides.

Oscar Roberts (10)
Forres Sandle Manor School

Happiness

When I think of all the times
When I am happy,
It feels like I'm in Heaven;
The big luminous sun,
The warmth on my face,
All my friends say that my eyes glisten,
Like two huge diamonds,
Sparkling in the sky above us.
It reminds me of when I am with the turtles,
Bubbles of happiness everywhere.
It looks like everyone is smiley, happy and joyful.
It feels like stroking a bunny rabbit,
Its tender fur tickling my fingers.
It smells like a breeze on a mid-winter's night.
And one day
When I am old and dying,
I will remember all the times when I was laughing,
Keeping all those memories tight inside my heart.

Jessica Davies (10)
Forres Sandle Manor School

Wonder

Wonder is a stream,
Trickling gently away.
Wonder never knows where it's going,
But it never stops.
Wonder feels like feathers,
Brushing gently across my face.
Wonder sounds like a waterfall,
Smashing the rocks far below.
Wonder is turquoise,
The turquoise sky on a sunny day.
Wonder smells of fresh flowers,
When they've just been picked.

Poppy Bolton Carter (10)
Forres Sandle Manor School

Joy

Joy is the colour of oranges
Growing on trees in the middle of spring
With blossom around
It tastes of sparkling pomegranate juice
In tropical restaurants of the Caribbean
It sounds like waves smashing the surf
As children shriek with laughter
As it tickles their toes
Joy looks like girls and boys flying kites
At the foot of a hill in the sunshine
Joy feels like a warm hug
That's been waiting for you for days on end
Joy smells like freshly baked bread
That's just come out of the baker's shop
Joy reminds you of your best friend
Playing with you in the playground
Joy is you having the best time
Of your life.

Ella Rowe (10)
Forres Sandle Manor School

Frustration

Frustration feels like something has just destroyed
All of your hopes
Say if you were put in a swim team
And you just got an injury
It sounds like someone yelling at you
'Go faster!'
'Work faster!'
When you are trying your hardest
It tastes like a bitter sherbet lemon
There are ups and downs to it
The colour of frustration is red.

William Hall (10)
Forres Sandle Manor School

Love

Love is red,
Like a heart pounding out of your chest.
Love is pink,
Like roses over the arch that the bride and groom walk under.
Love smells like a field of spring flowers,
Like freshly cut wedding cake.
Love sounds like the bells of a church,
Like a baby crying for the first time.
Love looks like a beach in Spain,
Like a romantic meal at an Italian diner.
Love feels like a big hug,
Like a kiss on the cheek for the first time.
Love reminds me of my first hug with my dad,
Of sitting on my own in my garden by the bamboo,
Listening to the birds cheeping.
Love tastes of Green & Blacks dark chocolate,
Of candyfloss.

Hannah Fearon (10)
Forres Sandle Manor School

Terror

You get a rumbling in your tummy,
Like a steam engine shaking the ground.
You go stiff, as if you were paralysed.
There's a burning fire in your head that you can't put out.
It smells like something that just died.
It reminds you of bad dreams,
You can't control it.
It shoots up your throat like you're going to throw up.
It tastes like a dry burnt piece of meat.
It's a very dark colour that only makes scary things visible;
You can't think of anything,
Except for the thing that might be coming down your corridor . . .
Boo!

Charlie Savage (10)
Forres Sandle Manor School

Love

Love is like a red rose,
That has been picked out of a green meadow.
It makes me think of my family,
And happy times that have happened in my life.
Love is a kiss,
That stays in my heart forever.
It makes me joyful and happy,
It never makes me lonely or sad.
All it makes me want to do
Is snuggle up under a warm duvet.
Love is red,
Like red cherry lips that have just kissed someone.
It reminds me of when my Aunty Amanda
Told me she was engaged.
Love gives me courage, and hope.
It is always peace, never war.
Love is a hug from the heart.

Laura Wyles (10)
Forres Sandle Manor School

Courage

Courage feels like giving someone the chance to stand up to
Someone like a bully
It keeps a friendship together, without falling
Courage's colour is a red colour
Which can mean determination to sort things out
Courage sounds like someone comforting a person
Who is crying
Courage looks like people helping each other
Courage reminds me of my friends.

Alexander Brown (10)
Forres Sandle Manor School

Boredom

Boredom is the colour of black,
The dullest colour.
It smells of absolutely nothing.
It tastes like a hard boiled sweet
Just sitting in your mouth.
It sounds like a teacher explaining a test.
It looks like a test paper sitting on the desk.
It feels like a ten tonne weight
As you're holding it.
It reminds me of all the times I'm sitting in the classroom
Not knowing what to do
Because I wasn't listening
And I felt sleepy.
Boredom is when I look inside my head
And nothing's there.

Hugo Campbell-Smith (11)
Forres Sandle Manor School

Pain

Pain is red,
The colour of blood,
Oozing out of your body.
Pain tastes like freshly picked sour lemons.
Pain sounds like the screaming and crying of untold agony.
Pain smells like red-hot metal on a fire.
Pain feels like mean words being slapped in your face.
Pain looks like a child curled up trying to protect itself.

Bella Skeates (10)
Forres Sandle Manor School

Pain

Pain is red, like the Devil doing bad.
Pain sounds like screams and cries in the distance.
Pain feels like a sting that you can't escape.
Pain smells like the burning of wood.
Pain reminds me of all the bad things that have happened.
Pain looks like darkness enveloping you.
Pain tastes like the sourness of a lemon.

Luke Robinson (10)
Forres Sandle Manor School

Hope

Hope is a light shining in the distance,
Gleaming and opening up the world.
It tastes sweet and smells like unfurling roses.
It feels like a warm and comfy bed
That you have been searching for your whole life.
And it reminds me of seeing my dog as a puppy
Fast asleep in my arms.

Samuel Everard (10)
Forres Sandle Manor School

Joy

The sight of joy is someone proud.
The sound of joy is someone laughing out loud.
The smell of joy is fresh herbs and flowers.
The feel of joy is something you've been waiting to touch for hours.
And the taste of joy is something sweet, a bit like sherbet,
What a treat!

Theresa Allsopp (10)
Forres Sandle Manor School

Life In School

The delightful pond
With frogs leaping
Back and forth,
And the tadpoles
Evolving into
Slimy green frogs
Like their parents,
And the water
Like frozen juice
Melting in the sun.

Then the pigeons
Start having a good natter,
When they're finished
They fly from one tree
To the next,
And then swooping down
And snatching
Ten long juicy worms
In their bulky beaks.

The lavender smelt like
A fresh cake
That had just
Come out of the oven,
And the leaves crumbled
Down like an old castle
Falling down,
And dropped on the
Solid ground,
Then I saw new
Life within death.

William Parsons (10)
Grey House Preparatory School

A Summer's Day

Marigolds, the golden guards,
Protecting the others.

The cyclamen are running,
Trying hard to win the race.

The grass,
As green as emeralds,
The blades brightening up the day.

The sparrows,
Swifts and blackbirds,
Tweet to their heart's
Delight.

The ivy creeps
Up the walls,
Climbing up Mount Everest.

As the nasturtiums
Go to sleep,
In someone's stomach!

Jonathan Boyce (10)
Grey House Preparatory School

Sports Hall

S hiny, sparkling, new - the sports hall stands on stone slabs,
P recariously balanced on the aerial sits a scarlet-red robin,
O ver the back of the hall dark, damp sap seeping off the wood,
R eddy-brown streaks of sap running down,
T he deflated ball popped on a razor-sharp thorn,
S tone slabs sparkling surrounds the hall as if it were a lake.

H appy is what I feel inside,
A lways the hall seems bigger,
L arge, larger, largest, huge, it's giant,
L ove of our new sports hall never stops.

Oliver Amatt (10)
Grey House Preparatory School

Curry

The pumpkin in the sun glowed
Like a lantern with a freshly lit candle.

The sweet potato was rough
Like an unused piece of sandpaper.

The courgette shone
Like an emerald at the bottom of a river.

The rice crackled
Like a box of popcorn.

The chilli spat fiercely
Like a raging campfire.

The pepper sizzled
Like chicken on a spit.

The sauce bubbled gently
Like a soothing hot spring.

The curry was served
And we all tucked in.

Benjamin Amatt (10)
Grey House Preparatory School

The Secret Garden

The hedges loom,
Making a shelter from the sunlight,
Hiding a garden as subtle as an ocean.

As the early morning sun
Glints magically off the soft, dewy grass,
Butterflies flutter beautifully,
Bees buzz lazily,
And a gentle croaking noise
Emits from toads,
Who are hungrily awaiting flies.

Robert Cootes (10)
Grey House Preparatory School

Happiness

Happiness is eating a chip
Or giving someone a tip
Happiness is going on holiday
Or enjoying the springtime in May

Happiness is learning to whistle
Or tying your shoes for the first time ever
Happiness is meeting a friend and playing lots together
But happiness is listening to your feet in the white crunchy snow

Happiness is climbing a tree, sharing a secret
Or playing your drum in your own school band
Or winning a race and hearing your friends cheer, it's grand
Happiness is being alone
Or coming home

Happiness is baking a cake
Or sitting by a lake
Happiness is being part of a team
But happiness is also a free ice cream.

Alisha Windeatt (8)
Grey House Preparatory School

The Spider

The speckly spider, spinning its web
Which dazzles in the fresh morning dew,
Then, once finished, it waits for the
Bewildered fly that strays into its net,
He flies into the trap and the spider
Silently scuttles towards him,
Then all of a sudden, swish,
The spider is no more,
For a swallow has plucked it
From his sparkling web.

Reuben Chasey (10)
Grey House Preparatory School

Autumn

As the tender shining lemon-coloured sun
Sprinkles its rays amongst the juicy grass,
A spider spins its soft silken web
In the pretty autumn morning.

As the trees blow in the cool air
Their leaves floating down,
A robin sits on a moss-covered branch
Singing its morning song.

As a dormouse scuttles
Through dry crisp leaves,
Deep underground is a badger
Protecting his family.

As the petals of flowers
Blow in the wind,
It's autumn again.

Gemma Bertuzzi-Glover (10)
Grey House Preparatory School

Fresh Morning

Feeling the breeze of fresh air
Gently dropping on your face,
Watching the warm luminous glow of the sun
On a new day.

The purity of breathing in
Cold light air.

The clean little drops of water
Trickling off the tips of the petals
Calming me as I watch them.

Hearing the leaves scuttle
Across the ground,
Their reassuring sound, it soothes me too.

Joseph Allen (10)
Grey House Preparatory School

Happiness

Happiness is playing your clarinet for the first time,
Finishing your homework,
The last summer rose,
The crunch of the snow,
The smell of baking cakes,
And a nice summer breeze,
Autumn leaves falling off the trees,
Winning a race or coming home,
After a long day's work,
Getting presents for Christmas,
Having Easter on your birthday,
And getting sweets on Hallowe'en,
Keeping a secret,
Lots of surprises,
And meeting a friend you haven't seen for a long time.
That's happiness for me!

Amy Gower-Jones (8)
Grey House Preparatory School

The Daylight

As the wake of day lights the room
I creep down the stairs like a burglar
I open the unpainted, rusty, broken door
Then stepping outside, as the cold whispering wind snaps out
Like a lion snapping his teeth at his prey.

The old oak trees' leaves rustling like a packet of crisps
Then the shimmering bright and green grass sways side to side
Slowly, the sun melts like an ice cream
Then, spiky small animals creep out
And the big giant animals fall into a deep sleep.

The red sky fades as the darkness takes over
A fast flying yellow shooting star races across the sky
And his still friends say goodbye.

Anoushka Chandler (10)
Grey House Preparatory School

The Euonymus

The red petal falling to the ground,
On top of a pile of wet leaves.

The rough petal,
And its wet scaly skin sparkling in the daylight.

The whiff of perfume,
A tender smell of salt.

The taste of rough scales,
Touching my mouth.

I feel relaxed,
I feel like nothing is wrong in the world,
The anger has relinquished,
I hear the birds sing,
And the cars zoom past.

Timmy Galloway (10)
Grey House Preparatory School

The Airfield

The airfield, big and long,
Covered in tarmac,
Smooth like icing on a cake.

Rubber balls like marbles
Waiting to be pushed off runways,
Fuel ready to be used,
Shadowy hangars, hidden like
Black rocks in a swamp.

Jets asleep, engines off,
Crisp aerodynamics ready to make lift,
All edging to fly,
And waiting for war.

Alex Fraser (10)
Grey House Preparatory School

An Afternoon In The Garden

The lavender's drifting perfume,
Sweet though lemony and zesty.
The waxy leaves creak and sing,
While the spiders spin their deadly webs
And ignorant creatures fly deep within.

Some leaves are old, crispy and dry,
Though stained with a fiery crimson dye,
And the sweet piney smell of the conifers floating by.

The birds sing in the uppermost tree,
A beautiful song, a melody.
And the lark that swoops to catch its prey,
At the end of a long and tiring day.

Sophia Dugdale (10)
Grey House Preparatory School

Senses Awaken

A beautiful morning
To feel the gorgeous breeze of air
Brush past my body,
I can smell the lavender,
Strong and sweet as if honey
Had been dropped on it
Nasturtium petals taste sweet and spicy
And smell wonderfully strong
The beautiful blades of grass
Catch the light and send
Luminous sparks to my eyes
I can feel the calm, soft plant.

Jannik Mackel (11)
Grey House Preparatory School

Happiness

H appiness is the smell of cakes and happiness
   is getting presents.
A nd when you eat a chocolate bun you get a happy feeling.
P resents being unwrapped is what I really like.
P resents that come for my birthday is what I really like.
I like it when it snows in winter, that's what I like.
N ever will I not like chocolate, that's what I like.
E ndless days at school, that's what I like.
S ome pizza slices I put in my mouth, that's what I like.
S o what do you like?

Rosie Hudson (8)
Grey House Preparatory School

Unhappy

Not being with my dad
Not having a hamster
Being at school
Getting told off
Getting snowballs in my eyes
Having to be in a fit
Getting a 'no' from your parents
Losing sports games
Having an annoying little brother
Cold weather.

Ross Bandeira (9)
Grey House Preparatory School

Happiness

Happiness is eating a yummy cake
The smell of rosy red roses
Best friend is happiness
Dancing around under dewdrops
Happiness is opening presents under the Christmas tree.

The happiness of reading a new book
Giving something to someone you don't know
Happiness is just stopping and thinking and having a rest.
I just love happiness!

Sophie Fowles (8)
Grey House Preparatory School

The Garden

The lavender looks dead,
But in spring it will revive,
Autumn comes back, followed by winter,
And it will bring a gentle death.

The nasturtiums' orange petals glowing in the sun
And waving in the wind,
They may be good in some food,
They taste very spicy,
Their stems as green as the grass.

Alexander Polydorou (10)
Grey House Preparatory School

Happiness

H appiness is hearing and smelling bacon sizzling in the morning
A utumn leaves crunching underfoot when walking home
P ancake day, eating them with sugar and lemon
P ulling crackers with a loud bang at Christmas lunch
I like the smell of cut grass in the morning
N ice holiday, the flight and the holiday ahead
E nd of school term and having a long holiday before you
S now crunching underfoot while you walk to get your skis
S nowballs, falling from the sky and getting revenge.

George Griffiths (8)
Grey House Preparatory School

Happiness

H appy times are to love and share,
A nd Christmas, such a jolly time,
P laying with your very best friends,
P ulling joy out of those crackers at Christmas time.
I say goodbye to the summer roses, time for autumn leaves,
N o more homework, what a relief.
E very day happiness gets bigger.
S amaritans' purses are ready to give the children a lovely surprise.
S melling the cakes baking in the oven, ready to eat.

Isobel Warren (8)
Grey House Preparatory School

Happiness

Who says I can't be happy
When I am feeling blue?
Can't I just watch favourite films,
And then just go to bed?

Isn't there a trick to play?
Isn't there a joke to say?
Can't I burn some logs today,
And smell the smell of smoke again.

Keturah Bate (8)
Grey House Preparatory School

The Forest

The forest glinting in the moonlight,
An essence of sweetness lingers in the air,
Trees as tall as mountains,
A fox like an outcast looking for shelter.

Flowery smells wafted my way by the wind,
Leaves sway in the breeze,
The luscious plants drizzled with dew,
Snowdrops stand out in the sea of green.

Oscar Sutherland Dee (10)
Grey House Preparatory School

Autumn Falls

Moss-coated rock smells mouldy but tastes sour,
The spider on the web looks gorgeous and gleams in winter,
Behind the court, an interesting sound of birds and cars,
The old oak, a big proud tree, who looks like the king,
You hear the leaves brushing against the shed roof,
Nasturtium whistle when you put them to your mouth
And taste peculiar.

Ellen Wilkins (10)
Grey House Preparatory School

Happiness

Happiness is a free ice cream and coming home
at the end of the day.
Happiness is the colour of autumn leaves
and the smell of a cake baking.
Happiness is finishing your homework
and seeing my dog Lester.
Happiness is Christmas and snow falling.
Happiness is the smell of cut grass.

Ben Spratley (9)
Grey House Preparatory School

Happiness

Happiness is the smell of rain, cakes cooking, autumn leaves.
Winning a race, doing something good, the crunch of snow.
Happiness is when a clown says a joke to you.
The fun of finishing your homework, having fun at a party.
Having Christmas, *all* those presents.
Hallowe'en, jumping out and scaring people.
Easter, all those eggs.
Last of all, coming home and being loved by *God!*

Amanda Clark (8)
Grey House Preparatory School

The Green Ivy Bush

The ivy smells of the fresh morning air,
with curvy white lines in the centre,
and dark green in colour.

The bush cocooned with leaves,
twinkling in the morning sunlight,
glowing in the night's cold.

William Loten (10)
Grey House Preparatory School

Endless Trees

The trees towering over the dead flowers
The tall grass glistening in the sun
The smell of flowers engulfs me
The old oak standing proud on its own
The thick bushes not allowing light to come through
And the rows of endless trees.

Angus Carver (10)
Grey House Preparatory School

The Magical Land Of Gemini

The sun was shining on my back as I scurried along the beach
Trying to find somewhere to stay.
A shark tooth house appeared on the horizon.
The tension built up inside me.
The eerie sounds of the waves stayed inside my head.

An abandoned island with a coral reef was named Gemini.
Fear, fright and fun were circling my head.
The place made my hair stand on end.
The never-ending stairs went across the water and all around
The island.
It was mysterious, explosive and exciting.
A snake-skinned ramp went down the cliffs
Turning left and right.
I went through cold and dull caves, exploring the island.

Floating bridges, strange people and sea water as cold as ice.
The rocks were slippery and as big as boulders.
I love exploring but nothing has been like this.
Water like mirrors, rocks as big as houses.
I came across a bridge, I didn't know whether to cross it or not.
Then suddenly, cats' eyes lit up and I sprinted across
The magical floating bridge.
At the other side was a luminous house as big as a tepee.

Daisy Folland (10)
Heathfield Junior School

The Magical Land Of Calland

The magical land, the mystical land.
There are rocks thousands of years old,
But smooth and not worn out.
A man appears, he beckons me to follow him.
His white beard flapping in the wind
As he runs across the small yellow bridge.
In the corner there is a giant tooth or tusk.
I stay a bit longer, I cross the bridge,
He is not there, only more bridges.
As I make my way across the bridges
I near the colossal tooth or tusk.
And it is slowly vibrating.
I look below and see a sight to behold,
A little house, connected to the lock but above the water.
I soon get down there.
A bridge connected to the house and the rocks.
I go on the bridge to the house
But I am feeling weary after my long journey.
No bed in there, but there is the man.
'Why are you here?' he asks with a frown.
I'm not listening,
I am looking around, everything is brown.
I look at the man, he disappears
All that is left is a fake beard.
The magical land, the mystical land,
Full of surprises that's where I am.

Nicholas David Donaldson (11)
Heathfield Junior School

The Creepy Castle

Walking across the creaky steps of the drawbridge,
Owls hooting with the petrifying thunder and lightning,
Gutters dripping as I approached the door,
The mice squeaked, the bats flapping their wings furiously.

Connor Regan (9)
Heathfield Junior School

The Magical Land

Gliding through the blue, cloudy skies
Rough, ragged rocks towering above me
Sound of ice cracking in the distance
Wind blowing my hair softly
Waves crashing against the sandy rocks
Long spiral staircase leading to a mammoth's tooth
Bright, curly bridge with tiny lanterns to the side
Unstable to walk on
Duck-shaped house with a mushroom-shaped roof
The rusty, wobbly door squeaks when the wind blows
The house was lit up and had steel doors and pane windows
People think magical people are in there
Since it is a magical day
There are more paths leading out
From the back of the colourful, dusty house
It feels like you are in a dungeon
A smelly, cold dungeon
Here is the magical house in front of me
I don't know what is going to go on
It is so creepy . . .

Matilda Tearle (10)
Heathfield Junior School

Magical Lands

Rigid bridge still stable from a million years ago!
Thin, narrow bridge leading to
The swirling, graceful waves on the other side.
Hard, grey, rough rocks smashing against each other.
Every two seconds *bang, bang*
The waves start hitting against the rocks.
Long, spiral staircases leading down
To the illuminous bright duckhouse.
The door is as colourful as a peacock
And as bright as the lovely sun.

Jack Gould (10)
Heathfield Junior School

The Magical Land

It was on a Caribbean cruise.
When I was looking over the edge of the boat,
I saw the sun dancing like diamonds across the water,
Suddenly I went into a daydream and fell over the edge,
When I awoke, I found myself in a place,
I was on a magical island.
The water was as hot as the scorching sun.
It touched my feet, it made me feel warm inside.
It felt like a desolate place, not a soul to be seen.
The bridge was as creaky as an un-oiled gate.
It led me to a house floating on water.
I was scared, I thought I was going to fall in the blue crystal-
Clear water.
I looked at the dark blue and mint-green house.
It looked like a peacock's feathers,
My heart beat 1000 beats a minute.
I got to the front door, I felt the chills all round me,
I shivered in fright, what was I going to discover?

Elishia Robinson (11)
Heathfield Junior School

The Magical Lands

At the magical land,
You can make anything with sand,
On the boat,
You can go up in the sky and float,
When you get to the end of the big slide,
You start to glide,
When you jump off the swings,
You'll grow wings and you'll fly,
When you go on the climbing frame,
You won't have to hold on it
To climb the frame,
And that will be the most exciting adventure *ever!*

Kieran Baker (11)
Heathfield Junior School

The Magical Land Of Oz

Parachutes gliding all over the sea
Mysterious, magical man crept around the boulders silently!
I stumbled down the rough rocks and then . . .
I discovered a river with a winding rope bridge on it.
The sounds surrounding me, *whoosh, coo, coo. Shh.*
The night was gloomy.
I was by a bridge.
By it stood a house,
The lights were beautiful.
I made my way across the bright beautiful bridge.
On either side was dark gloomy water,
Which made me feel sick.
The house looked like a peacock.
It was all bright, colourful and decorated.
I went to the door, *is it rusty?* I thought
The door would creak like an un-oiled gate.
I stood at the door mysteriously
And wondered what in terror would happen next.

Jessica James (9)
Heathfield Junior School

Horrid Spook

Spooky, haunted house, with trees all around it,
A dark house with creaky doors,
Wobbly tree branches all around the house.
Dark black sky with blotches of white on the sky,
Bright light in the horrid house
And bits of green in the moonlight,
No birds can be seen in the sky,
Zombies live in the big, haunted house,
No sun can be found in the mystical, windy world,
Creaky door, big spooky bats and spiders inside,
The skies are grey.

Faith Parr (8)
Heathfield Junior School

The Magical Land

There was an old, ugly man
Who scurried across the stony cliffs and the ghostly bridges.
The rocks were as steep as a waterfall
So you had to be very careful,
Taking each step very slowly!
So were the bridges, they weren't very sturdy.
My brain was buzzing because of the deafening sound of
The waves crashing against the rocky cliffs!
The abandoned island was very peaceful and quiet
So that was nice but I had nobody to speak to!
As I approached the meditating house,
Well that is what it looked like.
I started to go red in fright,
The tension was building up inside me!
As I got closer to the house with every step,
I thought I saw something like a wizard with ten eyes
Or a horseman with two heads,
What would it be? . . . Who knows . . .

Jack Wilson (10)
Heathfield Junior School

Rocky Island

Gliding across the gigantic island,
Going side to side, up and down.
The swaying water brushed gently against the dark, dull rocks.
Dark and beautiful, creepy bridge floating smoothly above
The shining water.
The magical, splendid rocks went deep into the luxurious sand.
Then a spectacular hut, the patterns as round as a cartwheel.
The ancient door as silent as an ant.
A wooden bridge! Old and unusual.
With little midget cars in them,
The wonderful waterfall splashed like a wild horse.

Callum Wolfe (10)
Heathfield Junior School

The Haunted House

The very haunted house, freaky and the open window
With the zombie looking out the window,
As the door is creaking as the trees fade away,
Lightning crashing on the floor,
The eerie clouds gather together.
The floor covered in holes
While bats flutter away and ghosts surround the house,
While the werewolves howl.
Windows crashing and the moon is full.
The door is locked while the boy tries to run away.
Trees rustle with the boy dead, and death arrives,
More zombies arrive, surrounding the house,
A haunted place where you get kidnapped,
Killed and go to Hell.
Blood everywhere inside, eerie clouds strike,
The floor shuddering like it's the end of the world!

Kevin Chung (9)
Heathfield Junior School

Potions Exploding

Potions exploding, nobody there, making you jump,
Beastly witches and nosy wizards'
Magical powers distract people,
Witches sneaking into your bedroom at night,
Wizards' mystical shooting powers,
Nobody can stop them.
It's midnight, people are asleep,
Lights turned on,
Rock solid walls have a cold feeling inside your heart,
Creaking doors, spooking yourself, rattling windows,
Graveyards stay still, no movement at all,
Candles flickering through the long, magical, dark mansion,
Movement, nothing is there.

Rhonwen Ellis (8)
Heathfield Junior School

The Magical Land Of Jelub

I was shipwrecked and now I am abandoned on an island.
Now I am anticipating unknown adventures.
As I walked across crispy sand, I felt a chill of excitement.
What was I about to discover?
It was as cold as Antarctica,
As I slowly walked across the narrow, bumpy bridge.
I felt the goosebumps all around me
And the tension built up inside me!
I stumbled across the steep, stony steps
And I spotted in the distance, a mysterious palace
That was surrounded by glittering water.
The palace was illuminated with light and bright colours.
But the fear stopped me from opening the door.

Samantha Bridle (10)
Heathfield Junior School

Ghostly House

G hosts come out and make the floor go *creak, creak, creak*.
H aunted house, witches, wizards, ghosts - help!
O ut at night, scary things happen.
S cary house, black and freaky, makes the floor go *creaky, creaky*.
T he house is haunted, beware!
L ights turn on by themselves.
Y ou hope not to be captured.

H orrified by windows, crazy bats flapping.
O ut comes the moon, the only light lit.
U gly witches and wizards.
S pooky house, ghosts about.
E ek! It's haunted in there!

Rebecca Sellwood (10)
Heathfield Junior School

House Of The Dead

Tonight is the return of the ghost and the zombie.
It is a gloomy night, there is a boy who is up for a fright.
He thinks it is fun, a funfair ghost train.
Then he opens the door, it is so dark
It looks like you're underground.
Suddenly the ghost sees him and says,
'Nobody has escaped for 50 years.'
So the boy runs out of the house.
Then in his room the zombie is waiting.
For a mouse bit the zombie right on the leg.

Freya Whyte (9)
Heathfield Junior School

Witches Only Come Out At Night Or Do They?

Cat is stretching by the window with spider webs all over.
The arch by the door is creaking and sounds like it is falling.
All the trees are rustling together and making a spooky sound.
There is a witch that is cackling on her broomstick outside.
The witch swooped down to the door and bashed her fist
on the door.
The girl answered the door and no one was there,
All you could see is the moon shining bright.

Claire Anne Holmes (9)
Heathfield Junior School

Magical Lands

Rotten, gigantic rocks getting crushed by waves
And crumbling apart, waves coming in every 2 seconds
And battering rocks.
Deep, diamond, blue waves,
Wizards turning people into frogs with their fake bridge.
Long, winding bridge curly through the rocks and paths.
As colourful as a rainbow, the door can't be any brighter
Or it would blind my eyes.
Slowly and quietly I sneak through the door to see who it is.

Jack Fenna (10)
Heathfield Junior School

The Magical Land

The water glimmered as shiny as glimmering metal.
The mysterious, magical man crept around as silent as a mouse.
I stumbled down a rocky path,
Which led me to a house floating on water
As cold as a broken heart.
The rocky, rumbling path was as long as a long magical wand.
I wondered how I would get across it.
I was as frightened as can be.
The house looked as if nobody was ever going to come in it.

Nabila Jalil (10)
Heathfield Junior School

Untitled

Drifting in by a huge boat, on the calm, clear water.
Surrounded by the powerful, grey rocks and cliffs.
An unstable bridge that leads to a duck-shaped house
Floating on the calm, smooth water.
A bright, crystal, gold door with mysteries behind!
A password is needed or you will *die!*

April Street (10)
Heathfield Junior School

Magical Lands

Sharp, jagged rocks leaning over the salty blue ocean.
Blushing sun shining over half the land
While all the animals are burning.
Colourful house leading to an unstable, jagged bridge
With shark-infested water next to it.
Train track bridge with a multicoloured bridge
Since it was built in 1594.
A deserted land never discovered with no animals or humans
And has a new house, shaped like a duck.

Tyler Keith Humphry (10)
Heathfield Junior School

The Magical Land

A mystical land,
No one knows who lives there but . . .
Suddenly a man swoops across the big, bumpy bridges,
Will he find his way back?
Will he succeed?
No flowers, no plants,
Where will he live?
A pretty little house maybe?
Colours like a peacock's feathers.

Phoebe Fulcher (8)
Heathfield Junior School

The Unicorn

The unicorn, as white as the whitest ghost
The rainbow, as shiny as the whitest unicorn
The pebbly floor like the unicorn's horn
The sky as ghostly as can be
The spooky trees as spooky as can be
The background as spooky as the spooky ghost.

Millie Sturgess (9)
Heathfield Junior School

The Mess Island

Arriving on the mystery island.
With a *smash* and a *bang!*
Ancient mess from time to time.
Glistening, rotting grime on walls.
Fun and happy, mystical too.
Happy smiles everywhere, round and round they go.
Fly here, fly there, cheerful sounds everywhere.
Nothing bad happens here.
Always sunny on Mess Island.

Leyla Ozgul (9)
Heathfield Junior School

The Magical Land Of Mist

Swirling sweetly in circles.
Mysterious music with windy sounds.
A small hat-shaped roof on a shimmering, shiny building.
Swirling, whirling bridges leading to different places.
Tall, towering boulders stacked.
A tall tooth-shaped building with a small window.
A man scurried silently across the short, sparkly bridge.
The door looked welcoming like a crocodile's grin.
Slippery, slidy rocks all over the place.

Cally Summer Webb (8)
Heathfield Junior School

Magical Land

Flying through the majestic, clear skies
An old, rusty bridge leading to some colossal, dirty rocks
Calm, gloomy water swirling silently around a house
A long, illusional bridge
A house like a penguin's head
Lots of windows like a prophecy.

Kiriana Oliver (9)
Heathfield Junior School

The Haunted House

The sky was black and scary.
The bats were flapping, loud and creepy
At the top of the haunted, scary house.
It was thundering.
Nobody had lived at that haunted house ten years,
With broken windows, broken rooftops and broken floors.
With nine ghosts in the house.
24 people got trapped in the house
And they didn't manage to get out of this haunted house.

Audrey Lam (9)
Heathfield Junior School

Magical Lands

Huge cliff looking down onto a wobbly bridge
With water, 1000 metres deep.
An uneven bridge like a train track.
Stifling hot sun sizzles us to a crisp like bacon.
Lights leading me to a shelter,
Floating on cool sparkling water,
Waves lap on to the elf's house.
An elf house like a new magic land, all colourful.
A teeny tiny man as green and old as the Grinch.

Lauryn Garner (10)
Heathfield Junior School

Magical Land

I silently swooped down to the rough, rugged rocks
There was a bright bridge that led to a colourful house
A man ran over the bumpy, broken bridge
The creepy front door was on a colourful, pretty house
The colourful, misty house belonged to a creepy wizard
Who turned people into frogs.

Holly Tinney (8)
Heathfield Junior School

Magical Lands

We soar above the land silently,
A tattered and dusty bridge
Leads to lots of mysteries.
A gigantic, old bull mammoth tusk
Stands on an endless canyon.
A long, rusty train track
Leads to a snake-like bridge.
The door to the strange house with the fungus roof
Is as colourful as a peacock's tail.

Lucy Greenfield (10)
Heathfield Junior School

Magical Lands

The huge boat takes us to
The old prehistoric land with no food.
The people are hardly alive,
The sea is as crazy as a monster.
The bridge is floating but you can't walk across,
You have to fly across.
The door is as blue as the sky.
The house looks undisturbed,
I wonder what's behind the door.

Reegan Byrne (8)
Heathfield Junior School

Wizard

W ise old man of magic
I n a land far away
Z igzags of lightning
A bove the world so high
R acing his powers with trembling hands
D readful wizard loves his magic!

Bayleigh Wicks (9)
Heathfield Junior School

The Magical Land!

Blue, empty sky up above the mystical land.
I felt the cold breeze on my face.
Rocks as knobbly as a toad's back.
Never-ending cliff faces just dropping down and down.
Huge, tooth-shaped house looming in the distance.
Light-guided path leading to the small house.
The crystal ice bridge floated effortlessly on top of the clear blue water.
Rusty, rotten railway line floated magically in the air.

Brooke Rennie (10)
Heathfield Junior School

Arriving At The Island

Arriving on the island with a bang.
Shaky bridges.
A hippy van floating in the air.
A creepy breeze running through my hair.
The lovely sound of the sea.
The smell of smelly seagulls.
The amazing sound of fairies.
Diamonds shining in the sky.
Bunnies jumping around, around on the road.

Jamie Gray (10)
Heathfield Junior School

The Magic Land Of Old England

The stony, slim path shaking when you step on it.
Waves crashing on old crumbling rock from prehistoric times.
The water as calm as classical music.
Mist over the water, who knows what is in it.
Exotic fruit growing on monstrous trees,
Taller than Mount Everest.

Owen Crook (10)
Heathfield Junior School

The Magical Land Of The Mysterious World

The grey, gloomy rocks around the island.
A very scary bridge, which goes into the water.
When anything treads or goes in, it will fall into the blue water.
Silver, shiny lights, which shimmer into the crystal-clear water.
A glittery, light bridge which leads to a magical, mysterious house.
The door is as beautiful as a butterfly.
A man swooped silently around the corner then across the bridge.

Jade Leah Mason (9)
Heathfield Junior School

A Magical Freaky Night

The bats are shimmering the dusky sky.
It is all quiet near the haunted house.
A bright light comes on
And there is a dark gloomy shadow
Shaped as a frightening ghost.
The sun is starting to rise and getting bright.
The haunted house path has started to glow like the sun.
The trees are starting to shake because of the wind.

Abbie Sketcher (10)
Heathfield Junior School

Haunted House

The bats swoop through the air past a spooked mansion.
Spirits appear from the misty sky.
As a ghost hovers through the wall.
Lightning thunders, stairs creaking,
Broomsticks leaning against a wall.
A few seconds later, gone!
Sweeping its way out the door.

Drew Taylor (9)
Heathfield Junior School

The Magical Land

I glided gracefully across the crashing wavy sea.
The crystal ice bridge floats calmly
across the glimmering, shiny water.
Never-ending spiral staircase winds up to nowhere.
A bridge as sparkling as a wizard's dust.
Calm, settled water as cold as a broken heart.
A mysterious, monstrous man
hiding silently in the shadows of the cliffs.

Taya Byrne (10)
Heathfield Junior School

Dracula

D racula in front of the huge white moon
R *ing, ring* at the door
A visitor to stay tonight
'C ome in,' Dracula whispered
U nlikely, Dracula ripped the man to shreds'
'L ovely, I haven't had anything to eat in ages
A fter the man's soul produced, Dracula caught him
  and stuck him in a dark place.

Marcus Talbot-Roe (9)
Heathfield Junior School

The Magical Land

An illuminous house in the dusk,
As I soar through the air as still as rust.
Fierce waves crashing against the soft, silent sand.
How many miles left will I be able to stand?
Glowing lights, like fairies dancing on the plains.
How long will it be when the heavens open up and rain?
Cold, settled water as cold as a broken heart.
I am alone.

Anna Townsend (10)
Heathfield Junior School

Ghosts Are Everywhere

The cobwebs outside her house are getting bigger by the hour.
Bats are sweeping down one by one.
Witch stirring a potion, she reaches out and grabs a bat
To put into her potion.
The girl inside the spooky house is getting ready to go to bed
When there is a knock at the door, the ghost is smiling at her.
The pond outside her house is splishing and sploshing
As the creepy toads and fish are jumping out of the pond.

Jessica Rose Cornwall (9)
Heathfield Junior School

Starry Night

Rainbow as shiny as the sun.
Stones as colourful as a rainbow.
The sky is as glittery and colourful as a unicorn.
The unicorn is as shiny as the pebbly floor.
The background is the best thing
I have ever seen in my life.
On the end of the unicorn
There is a shiny, glittery star.

Katie Lumb (9)
Heathfield Junior School

The Magical Land Of Mist

I flew gracefully into the magical, misty land
Underneath all the rocks there were gleaming lights
There was a peacock-like house over a floating bridge
That stood there silently
Rocky beaches as huge as a wizard's cave
It was a rocky land like never before
The door on the house was as beautiful as a butterfly
Silver, shining lights gleamed everywhere.

Indigo Amelia Muirhead (10)
Heathfield Junior School

Magical Land Of Georgia Freeman

The cloudy, deserted, misty sky is so gorgeous.
The gargantuous shark's tooth is really a . . . cave.
The bright long bridge is unstable to go on.
The bridge is as curly as a Curly Wurly.
On the cold, wavy water you can see
Your fantastic, beautiful reflection.
The exotic, grand house is only for posh people.
The deep, blue sea rippling on me.

Georgia Freeman (9)
Heathfield Junior School

The Spooky Magical Land

A rocky blue water really deep
And an old huge tooth
At this time I feel spooked out
And like someone was watching me.
Can you hear birds singing
And peoples' music playing.
The sinky bridge on top of the water
If anyone stepped on it, it will sink.

Rhys Rannochan (11)
Heathfield Junior School

Candy Land

A little land full of sweets is strange to see
The people here are mini, spotty and blue
They walk by a strange, little house with ice cream on top
A waterfall flowing down to the river
The food is great, they don't only eat candy even though
There's plenty
This is a place where magic begins.

Lisa Chung (10)
Heathfield Junior School

Haunted House

Spooky, mystical and mystery
The haunted house will shock you to *death!*
Eerie calls from the werewolves
Fill the misty air.
Fresh, rich blood
Makes its way through the crooked door.
Ah ha, ha, ha!

Sapphire Lewis (9)
Heathfield Junior School

Magic

M agic is cool
A nd people have fun with magic
G ood is fun
I will be amazing at magic
C ool magic
A ll I want to do is magic
L ovely fairies flying around.

Stacie Lovell (10)
Heathfield Junior School

The Magical Land

Silently we flew to the magical land.
A sharp, spooky, tooth-shaped building.
There was a crystal ice bridge too shiny to look at.
A mysterious, magical, moonlit bridge.
The peacock house glistened across the water.
Suddenly I felt as cold as a broken heart.
The moon slowly, silently slid behind a cloud.

Abigail Harker (9)
Heathfield Junior School

Fairies Come Out At Night

F airies come out at night when the moon is shining so bright.
A wonderful fairy glows when stars come out and it's all peaceful and quiet.
I n the night they love to dance in the moonlight.
R ainbow in the sky, how the fairy loves you so.
Y ou are all wonderful fairies when you come out at night and play in the moonlight.

Hannah Kim Dowse (9)
Heathfield Junior School

Haunted House

Bats flying softly in the misty sky
Ghosts wandering slowly around the crackling house
Trees standing tall and scary in the midnight sky
Moon as bright as a light in the night sky
Gates as sharp as a pin in front of the castle wall
Bricks crumbling to the floor
As I walk past the scary house of doom.

Paige Ballard (9)
Heathfield Junior School

Magical

M erlin was a wizard
A nd he lived in a spooky cave
G ives any help if they need it
I n a land far, far away
C at in his hand as fat as a pancake
A s a haunted cave
L ikes to make nasty spells.

Ryan Cole (9)
Heathfield Junior School

Land Of Treats

Hocus pocus,
Giant cookies say hi,
Raining buttons fall from the sky,
Ice cream stands they're all so still,
Ice cream melts, just for a thrill,
    Hocus pocus,
      Goodbye.

Jack Marlow (10)
Heathfield Junior School

Fairy Town

M y world is magical and pink.
A nd Megan's is the same.
G ifted with a nice spell.
I 'm so glad I came up with it.
C ome on in to fairy town.
A nd everyone will love it like me.
L oved by everyone.

Jade Chappell (10)
Heathfield Junior School

Wizard

W izard in the dark night
I nteresting news spells come every day
Z *ing, zoop, zat* turn into a bat
A cockroach, spider, bat and sloppy slugs
R ats scavenging for food
D ark bats in the dark, beautiful night sky.

Henry Tearle (9)
Heathfield Junior School

Magical Land

Illuminous, pink peacock colours on the munchkin house.
Ice cracking deep into the cold, solid ground.
Scorching hot sun reflecting on to our bare bodies.
Dark, grey clouds hovering around the bright, illuminous sun.
Scorching hot sun right next to the fluffy, puffy clouds.

Courtney Eagle (10)
Heathfield Junior School

Magic

M agic, magic I love magic
A bracadabra
G azam, I'll be a magician
I 'll be a magician, how about you?
C at on a broom, I can see it go zoom.

Luke Heather (10)
Heathfield Junior School

Magical Land

White, misty fluffy cloud in the beautiful, blue sky.
Old, ancient city in the middle of nowhere.
Immense rocks fill the place in silence.
Freaky, old, rusty house like a duck.
Door as colourful as a peacock.

George Bowers (9)
Heathfield Junior School

Our Future

Wow . . .
I've just got back from the future!
And I'm feeling really dizzy!
Because I was travelling speedier!
Than the fastest Ferrari in the world!

In the future . . .
To get around from A to B
You hover like a bumblebee
Home from school on your hover board
At four, just in time for tea!

In the future . . .
You must go to the zoo!
Because then you will see a pele-raph-foxy-roo
Which is part pelican, giraffe, fox and kangaroo!
But don't worry 'cause the cows still say, 'Moo!'

In the future . . .
3D televisions are in every room
You lift your hand to raise the volume!
But the best of all is . . .
You can have them in the bathroom!

In the future . . .
Kids don't do homework anymore!
Robots do it! They don't get bored
Of maths or literacy or science books!
If you ask them nicely they will even cook!

In our future . . .
The colours of the rainbow haven't changed!
Blue, yellow, orange or red!
And our future will be green!
But only if we keep our planet clean!

Aamir Hamza Rajput (8)
Highfield CE Primary School

Paint Brush

I'm good at art
But when I was 10
I had more spare time to paint in
Now I remember the story
Of my very first paint set

I had great fun
Painted a mini Da Vinci
Yeah.
All of those details
Colours
Shades
Were on my paper
Masterpiece.

Little bit of blue paint needed here?
Reach!
Clang!
Splosh!
It's soaking
My school clothes - slimy and wet!
The table - expensive, now ruined!

'Your school clothes!
My table!'
My parents.
'I can't believe this, what's happened!' they chorus.
My catchphrase, 'I don't know.'
'You don't know!' they chorused.
'Your pocket money's being used on new school clothes!
You're making a new table!'
Not a great ending to my story.

Maggie Foster (10)
Highfield CE Primary School

Shoe

Shoes, shoes, shoes.
When I was 9,
I got in trouble for losing expensive pairs of shoes.
Once I lost my dad's signed football boots.
I was playing football, with my dad's precious football boots.
Flick, shoot, score, 'Wahoo!'
But then one of Dad's shoes was gone!
The strong smell of fresh leather had blown away,
I tried looking for it everywhere,
The next day I went to Rosie's house,
I told him what had happened.
He had an idea,
I painted one of my giant shoes black,
I hoped that Mum or Dad wouldn't notice.
But . . . but . . .
I think I forgot something,
Oh no I forgot the sign,
And Mum had already looked on the shoe shelf.
Oh no she didn't . . . oh yes she did.
She . . . she . . . took them to Dad,
'Michael!'
Uh-oh,
'What is this?' said Dad crossing his arms,
'Erm, er, I don't know.'
What a stupid thing to say.
'You don't know? How can you not know!
Right no answer, then no football for a month!'

Jimin Yim (9)
Highfield CE Primary School

Shoes

Shoes, shoes, shoes.
When I was 9
I got into very big trouble
With a pair of my dad's signed trainers.
At home, when Dad was out,
I tried on a pair of Dad's signed trainers
But accidently flicked them down the stairs.
Flick! Whoosh! Bonk! Cool!
I got some friends and . . .
Flick! Whoosh! Bonk! Cool!
We got a chair and did it off that
Flick! Whoosh! Crash! Oops!
Dad's signed shoe, lost out the window!
Mum's new Mac on the floor in pieces,
And a window broken.
Uh-oh!
Mum and Dad!
'What have you been doing in here?
And where are my precious shoes!'
Dad always says that.
'Go to your room, now!'
'OK.'
You could hear Dad sighing,
Huff.

Ellie Lewis (9)
Highfield CE Primary School

My Futuristic Poem

Maybe in the future there will be
A new kind of plant waiting for us to see,
The stalk as purple as a ripe, juicy plum.
Petals shaped like golden, shiny stars
And little spikes to keep people away.

Maybe in the future there will be
Something new to help you with your homework.
Homeworkbot 3000 will correct your spellings,
Help you with your times tables
And write your stories for you.

Maybe in the future there will be
A snowstorm so we cannot see,
Hot, sunny days in the winter and
Cold, wet days in the summer.

Maybe in the future there will be
Hundreds of shops run by me
And in my shops there will be
Clothes and toys and jewellery,
To make you happy, it's all free!

Aimee Rayner (8)
Highfield CE Primary School

Our Future

What will our future become?
Our beautiful world is suffering!
We're cutting down trees, burning fuels,
Filling our world with rubbish.
Polluting the planet, hotter and hotter,
The terrible greenhouse effect.

What will our future become?
Our beautiful world is in danger!
The ice caps are melting, sea levels rising
Seasons changing, more extreme.
Droughts, famines, storms, hurricanes,
The tragic side effects.

What will our future become?
Our beautiful world can be saved!
We're reducing, reusing, recycling.
Wind power, solar power, being green.
Planting, walking, saving energy, a positive effect.

Olivia Manger-Webber (8)
Highfield CE Primary School

The Future

Last night I had a dream
I was 1000 years forward in the future
There were shops full of sweets
And High School Musical
Singing on the streets
The cars would fly
In the ruby-red sky
To meet the smiling sun.
But guess what?
The sun had a huge hat!
As I put on my thinking cap
Which makes you clever enough
To not go to school,
I've just heard a beeping noise
Getting louder and louder.
Slowly I woke up and I realised
It was my alarm clock.

Raluca Alexii (8)
Highfield CE Primary School

Our Big Future!

Our future is hidden,
Our future is waiting.

Life is one long journey,
Filled with adventures of excitement,
You lose, you make,
But you carry on.

Our future is hidden,
Our future is waiting.

The future with flying cars,
In the future we are on Mars.
They can work on Jupiter,
They can play on Neptune.

The shops made of gold, silver multi-pounds wood.
Our future is waiting.

Wozniarski Patryk (9)
Highfield CE Primary School

The Future

The future, the future, what's it going to be?

Maybe winged cars, or a flightless bee.
Aliens come down . . . and take over the world.
And dinosaurs come back to roam the Earth.

The future, the future, what's it going to be?

Bunnies turn pink and frogs turn blue?
Land joins up and sea joins too!
Fish won't breathe and neither will Man.

The future, the future, what's it going to be?

Chickens go *quack* and monkeys go *boo!*
Everything goes purple?
Surely this cannot be.

Chris Lotery (8)
Highfield CE Primary School

The Greedy Elephant

This is a greedy elephant

This is a hungry elephant
That ate a tiger

This is a greedy elephant
That ate a tiger
That ate a lion

This is a hungry elephant
That ate a tiger
That ate a lion
That ate a gorilla

This is a greedy elephant
That ate a tiger
That ate a lion
That ate a gorilla
That ate a chimp

This is a hungry elephant
That ate a tiger
That ate a lion
That ate a gorilla
That ate a chimp
That ate a croc

This is a greedy elephant
That ate a tiger
That ate a lion
That ate a gorilla
That ate a chimp
That ate a croc
That ate a man

This is a mega hungry elephant
That ate a tiger
That ate a lion
That ate a gorilla
That ate a chimp
That ate a croc
That ate a man
That ate a . . .
Burger!

Jake Baker (10)
Netley Abbey Junior School

The Cat

A slither of darkness streaks up the tree
Eyes gleaming in the gibbous moonlight
Prowls along the branch with care
And waits.

A spoonful of treacle melts from the branch
Eyes gleaming in the gibbous moonlight
Slinks along the wall with care
And waits.

Dawn is riding the sleeping rooftops
His golden cloak a jewel in the sky
His brilliant aura eliminates moonlight
Galloping the sky in radiant joy.

A soft marshmallow curls up in bed
Purring, content in the light of the room
Whiskers twitching in silent laughter
She sleeps.

But at night the cat has a life of her own.

Eleanor Serpell-Stevens (11)
Netley Abbey Junior School

Where Claire Where?

Where are you Claire? Oh where, oh where?
I stare as I wonder where
You're not in the hallway
You're not in bed
You're not in the cupboard
And you're not upstairs!

Where Claire, O where, oh where,
Oh where, oh where could you be?
I'm so frightened and so scared
I worry and I wonder
O where, o where could you be?

Where is that silly Claire?
I glare as I wonder where,
You're not in the bath
But you're wearing your scarf
Cos it's not in your room . . .

I know where you are
I know what to do
Because I told you to shoo!

I tiptoe outside to open the shed . . .
1 . . . 2 . . . 3!
Boo!
Guess what, I found you!

Abby Parker (10)
Netley Abbey Junior School

Darkness

Gloomy shadows drifting away into the darkness.
Raven skies swallowing up the last beam of a star.
Never-ending darkness as hollow as a willow tree.
A shiver runs down my spine,
Lifeless wolves howling at the glimmering moon.

Katie-Lynn Lucas (10)
Netley Abbey Junior School

Where's Monkey?

There's Monkey on his motorbike,
Going up the hill,
There's Monkey on the toilet,
Sitting very still.

Where is Monkey going now?

There's Monkey in his car,
Going too fast,
There's Monkey in the train,
Being a real pain.

There's Monkey in the tree,
He's going to fall,
There's Monkey in the bath,
Having a nice wash.

Where is Monkey going now?

There's Monkey in his bed,
Where is he going tomorrow?

Matthew Hooper (10)
Netley Abbey Junior School

In The Night

In the night I feel alone
Something's watching me, I look around
And yet I can't see.

A sunset is coming and cats are chanting
Something's rummaging around.
A slightest bit of darkness catapults into the sky
As I run my way home going ever so briskly.

While I lay in my bed I say to myself
What really goes on in the night?
But you and I know
That the bogeyman says, 'Boo!'

Charlie Felton (11)
Netley Abbey Junior School

My Loved Poem

Loved is a place that is warm
Like at Christmas or any special occasion.
Loved is who?
Anyone, it's a really lovely feeling to feel.
Where is loved?
Anywhere at any time,
It's a very deep feeling and
It's a very safe, cosy feeling!
Why is loved a feeling?
Because without that feeling you wouldn't feel
That your parents loved you
Which would be really horrible indeed!
Also you would feel neglected by your own mum and dad!
In what places do you feel loved?
Anywhere as long as everyone who's there loves you
Most likely your family!

Ella Purkiss (9)
Netley Abbey Junior School

My Lonely Poem

Lonely is a place
Where it's damp, dirty and quiet.
Like you're trapped in some dark, doomed prison.
When I am somewhere I hear people laughing
That used to be me.
Like it's in a tiny room
And I just feel like I am cooped up.
When it's cold you feel like you don't want to be there.
I want my friends to come with me
Because they make me laugh.
When it's spooky
You just feel like you don't want to be there.
I want to just disappear from everyone
Because I want to be on my own.

Amber Jones (7)
Netley Abbey Junior School

Skies

Mackerel sky, mackerel sky
Never long wet, never long dry
He who dares to hurt the mackerel sky
He will die
Some say it's blood, some say it's rubies
Some say it will cause a flood
The crimson sky never cares
But warns the shepherd of the weather to come
A black veil flew over the sun
Concealing its brightness
The ebony clouds engulfing the warmth
With its murky wisps forecasting a torrential downpour
God's face stood gleaming in the light
Surrounded by the azure silk
The white candyfloss clouds floated
Throughout infinity.

Ellie Nelson (11)
Netley Abbey Junior School

My Lonely Poem

Lonely is a place
Where you're left out and there's no one there
Like a damp cave
Lonely is no one there to talk to,
To play with never ever
But you might find someone one day.

When it's pitch-black
I want to have a friend to play with
And a light to help me see.

Lonely is a place
Where you have no one there
Like a tiny room all squashed up
Not anything like a prison.

Georgia Henry-Dobbyn (7)
Netley Abbey Junior School

My Teacher

Teachers are fantastically fun
They always have time for everyone
My teacher's really cool
He's taught at Netley and Poole
But when it comes to homework
I don't know what to say
Even though I hand it in almost every day
I guess they're a sort of mate
Who's absolutely great
 T errific
 E xcellent
 A lways fun
 C ool
 H appy
 E ager
 R espectful.

Jasmine Florence Dyer (9)
Netley Abbey Junior School

My Angry Poem

Angry is a place
Where it feels like I want to kick and punch
Like a deep, dark place

Anger is a place
Where it seems like no one loves you
Like under my stairs

When it's hot and sweaty
I want to cool down straight away

When it's dark and scary
I want to sit down and scream as loud as I can

Sometimes I want to be alone
And other times I want someone there.

Megan Victoria Elliott (9)
Netley Abbey Junior School

My Love Poem

Love is a place
Where I feel safe
Like my room when my mum comes in
To give me a hug and a kiss.

Love is a place
Where everyone loves me
Like when there's a party
With my friends and family.

When I'm sad and lonely
I want to shout, 'Help me!'
I want to crunch my hands
And shout even more.

When I'm loved I feel happy
And I want to be loved even more.

Ella Jane Clark (8)
Netley Abbey Junior School

My Upset Poem

Upset is a place
Where no one dares to go
That is cold and wet and miserable all around.

Upset is a place
Deep under the sea
Where no one lays
Their feet or breathes.

One day I just
Wish that I could
Just walk through air
Calmly and smoothly.

When I feel miserable
I wish I wasn't here.

Charlotte Captain (7)
Netley Abbey Junior School

The Butlock's Wood's Ghost

Deep in the woods dark at night,
The noises that surround me
Give me quite a fright.
The leaves crunching and creeping past
While I walk by
As if someone's by my side.
My worst fear,
I feel a ghost is near.
Shall I run away
Or should I stay
And risk the danger that's near?
I feel his breath on my shoulder,
Getting louder and louder.
I run to the entrance of the never-ending woods.
When I look I see the Butlock's ghost!

Leonie Bath (10)
Netley Abbey Junior School

The Woods At Night

The woods at night can give you a trembling fright,
The moon will shine and the light is terrifyingly bright.
The wolf will howl at the moon
And cry for his food . . . and you might just die!
The bats will screech and you will hear
The terrible noise in your ear.
You would run if you were smart
Because you wouldn't want to be torn apart.
The woods at night can give you a trembling fright,
The moon will shine and the light is terrifyingly bright.
The stench of the air is frightening, disgusting and sweet,
If you dare smell it you'll be knocked off your feet.
The time has come for you to go and I promise you will know
That if you leave you'll be grateful,
But if you don't your death is fatal.

Bethany Battle (10)
Netley Abbey Junior School

My Excited Poem

Being excited makes me feel like
I'm in a fantasy world
It's like everyone is surrounding me
And laughing at my jokes
Excited makes me feel like
I'm the most popular girl in the world
Sometimes I like to curl up in a ball
But they keep coming near me
I don't mind because I'm quite kind
And always will be
But when I feel blue
My mum and dad tell me that they love me
When it's a happy place
I feel like I want to go to space
With my mum, dad and my sister Jess.

Isabel Scott (8)
Netley Abbey Junior School

My Impatient Poem

Impatient is a place,
That seems far away.
Like down a well or in a long tunnel.

Sometimes I want to fast forward time,
But on other occasions I feel like waiting!

Impatient is a place,
That feels disturbing and waiting to make me burst.
Like the impatient feeling gets pushed away and longer.

When it's thick and deep,
I dare myself to go faster.

When it's thin and shallow,
I want to go far away.

Hannah Buckley (9)
Netley Abbey Junior School

My Fearful Poem

Fearful is a place
Where people try to talk but you run away
Like you want a cookie but you don't dare ask
You just stay where you are

Fearful is a place
Where you don't want to come down from your room
Because you don't want to show yourself to people

When it's scary and you don't show anywhere
You want to run away and never come back

When it's too frightful and you hate it
You want not to be here
You want to be gone!

Hannah Thompson (7)
Netley Abbey Junior School

My Happy Poem

Happy is a place
Where people are pleased
Like when you're at a party.

Happy is a place
Where everyone is pleased
Like at Christmas when everyone's pleased and overjoyed.

When I'm happy
I want to do anything that I enjoy
Like playing in the garage.

When I'm cheerful
I want to go up into the loft
And make a den.

Henry Hammond (8)
Netley Abbey Junior School

Txting Throo The Day

2day was gr8,
Even tho I was l8,
Drinking my t at hom

2gether 4ever,
Luv is 4ever,
Fanc a x from me.

4 t it's chips,
Wyl waching the ships,
Leving the dock 4 good.

I went 2 bed,
And bumpd my hed,
And stayd asleep 4ever.

Heather Robins (11)
Netley Abbey Junior School

My Angry Poem

Angry is a place
Where you are mad and stressy,
Like when you feel dead inside
And the good side disappears.

Angry is a place
Where you are annoyed
And you just want to lash out at them,
Like when someone is clinching your heart inside.

When it is strong and fierce,
I want to be alone and invincible.

When it is small and looking,
I want to yell and scream at them.

Matthew Benney (9)
Netley Abbey Junior School

The Sea

The sea is not lonely,
It has lots of friends,
Dolphins, fish and turtles.
But deep, deep down,
Inside a crack,
Lives a little sea horse,
Named Billy Crank!
Down below,
A beautiful mermaid,
Whose name is Princess Pearl.
But overall, everyone there
Loves to dance
And loves to share!

Ami Hewlett (10)
Netley Abbey Junior School

My Upset Poem

Upset is a place
That I don't like to be in,
Because it feels like a big rain cloud following me.

Upset is a place
Where I feel scared
Like in a deep dark hospital.
It's called misery.

When I imagine things in my head,
I feel really worried.
I just feel like
I want to scurry away like a mouse
Into safety.

Amber Parker (8)
Netley Abbey Junior School

The Sporting Trio

I am in the boxing ring
Waiting for Master Ming.
I am going to kick his butt
Because he is a major nut!

I am on a dark black horse
And my name is Inspector Morse,
Now I'm going to get 10 bucks
But my horse sucks!

I'm playing hockey
And I'm not a jockey,
Then I scored an awesome goal
But it hit the pole.

Alex Ings (10)
Netley Abbey Junior School

Trick Of The Eye

As I creep down the spiral staircase,
Creaking as I go,
My heart begins to pound and race,
The further I may go.

Tiptoeing down the hallway,
Towards the kitchen table,
Through the blink of my eye,
I can see the baby's cradle.

I edge forward seeing something,
Mysterious in my eye,
As I move forward I can see,
This is all a great big lie.

Anna Rogers (10)
Netley Abbey Junior School

My Excited Poem

Excited is a place
Where my tummy goes all funny
Like when I am waiting for my birthday to come.

Excited is a place
Where it's nearly Christmas Day
Like when I jump up and down and say yay, yay, yay

When it's not Christmas, a party or my birthday
I want to sit on my bed and think in my head

When it's nearly Christmas
I want to watch my Christmas tree shine
And wait for Santa to come in the night.

Daisy An Smith (8)
Netley Abbey Junior School

My Happy, Laughing Poem

When I'm happy and having fun
I feel all warm and special
Like I'm snuggling in my bed, cosy and happy.

I smile and laugh and my friend does that too
I love having fun with my friends and family
Who I love too.

We build dens and jump in the pool
We play on our DS and have fun in the garden
Or go on the trampoline and we even send messages.

It's nice having someone you can play with and rely on
Not lying, you should put a smile on.

Elyse Marshall (8)
Netley Abbey Junior School

My Happy Poem

Happy is a place
Where I can hear people laughing
In a swimming pool

Happy is a place
Where happy things happen
When you get your favourite toy

When it's happy
I want to have a party
Have a big cake

When it's snowing and I can go outside
I have a snowball fight.

Tomas Shacklady-Suarez (7)
Netley Abbey Junior School

My Exciting Poem

Exciting is a place
Where we play with our friends
At a theme park
And we see all the squirting waves go up and down.

Exciting is a place
Where you eat ice cream on a sunny day
It is fun, like gliding down a slide.

Exciting is a place
Where you tell jokes and go to McDonald's.

When I'm in an exciting place,
I feel so happy.

Jasmine Charles-Smith (8)
Netley Abbey Junior School

My Loved Poem

Loved is a place
Where inside you deep down
People love you because you're special
Everyone is special
Love is a place
Where you get to have fun
Like a dream in the sky
When it's around you
You want to stay in this world
I hope I do
Love travels around the world
I want to stay in this world forever.

Yasmin Paddon (7)
Netley Abbey Junior School

Cats

He slinks along the damp spring grass,
Looking for a spot to sleep,
At night he hunts for a mouse that might be,
Scurrying across his path,
He sits, he waits with caution,
Seeing his prey he pounces,
Catches his dinner and tumbles,
That's the end of our pygmy-pawed rodent,
He bundles back into the kitchen,
Snuggles up in his basket,
And when it comes to morning tomorrow,
He'll pounce on his owner to wake her.

Brooke Wilkinson (10)
Netley Abbey Junior School

Darkness, Light

Darkness will creep through the window
Even when it's closed.
Darkness will slide into nothingness
And regroup with its mates.
Darkness will turn air black
And freak people out!

Darkness here, darkness there,
Darkness will be everywhere!

Darkness will be a devil to some
But a powerful ally, darkness will lie.
Darkness has an enemy - *light!*

Andrew Pimm (10)
Netley Abbey Junior School

My Hungry Poem

Hungry is a place
Where there's no food around
And you are starving
Like you are trapped in a dark gloomy cave and very scared.

Hungry is a place
Where you're there flat on your bed
Like no one is there for you to give you any food.

When it's dark and gloomy
I want to just call a friend to set me free.
When it's a place where no one is there
I want to cry and eat something.

Ellie-Mae D'Ambrosio (8)
Netley Abbey Junior School

The Happy Deck: No Darkness Allowed! My Happy Poem

Happy is a place
Where down in the dumps never exists
Like all the amazing rides at Legoland.
Happy is a place,
Where it is high and light,
Like the shining sun that covers the planets
When it's starting to get great,
I want to take part in this epic chase.
And when it's reeling up darkness,
I want to show off happiness.

Joseph Cann (7)
Netley Abbey Junior School

My Gloomy Poem

Gloomy is a place
Where it's lonely and it hurts
Like at night where it is spooky and frightening.

Gloomy is a place
Where it's dark and cornered in a room
Like thunder and lightning.

When it's lonely and it hurts
I want to just disappear.

When it's dark and cornered
I want to be left back there.

Gabrielle Thorne (9)
Netley Abbey Junior School

My Upset Poem

Upset is a place
Where darkness lays
Like under a deep dark bed.

Upset is a place
Where needles pinch
Like a dark scary hospital.

When it's dark as night
I want to cuddle my teddy.

When it's cold
I want to hide under my covers.

Harry Robinson (8)
Netley Abbey Junior School

My Guilty Poem

Guilty is a place
Where it's inside, trapped in prison
Like detention, a place full of guilt.

Guilty is a place
Where immoral things are done
Like prison, illegal and shameful.

When it's dark and dim,
I want to fly away.

When it's phosphorous and light,
I feel welcome to have guilt.

Abigail Hooper (8)
Netley Abbey Junior School

My Happy Poem

When I'm happy,
I've got an excited feeling.
A happy place is Haskins
A happy time is
When you're at Haskins
Getting a hamster
A happy place is
Somewhere light and shiny
Like a moonlit night
A happy place is
With your family watching TV.

William Fox (8)
Netley Abbey Junior School

My Hungry Poem

Hungry is a place
Where it is dark and scary
Like you are trapped in a prison with lots of adults
When it's dark and scary
I want to ask someone to set me free
Hungry is a place
Where I can hear tummy rumbles
Like a restaurant that has run out of food
And has to get some more
When I can hear tummy rumbles
I want to go to another restaurant.

Millie James (7)
Netley Abbey Junior School

The Fireplace

It hasn't been lit for centuries.
People say it's haunted.
If you don't believe it then you're mad!
Go by it and you're gone.
People have gone and never come back.
The only thing that comes out it is dust.
When it's dark there's a small light,
That shines every night,
Some say it's eyes,
Others say it's falling stars,
What do you believe?

Chloe Cook (11)
Netley Abbey Junior School

Moonlight

You see the moonlight in front of you,
You wonder what's up there, is it you?
You see the light, it's blinding you,
It's just a ball of fire, isn't that true?

You see the moonlight in front of you,
The raven sky glaring at you.
You catch a drop of the misty rain,
Then the moonlight fading away!

You see the moonlight in front of you,
You stand and stare while it's burning at you . . .

Amy Blann (10)
Netley Abbey Junior School

My Sad Poem

Sad is a place
Where I don't have any friends
Like playtime

Sad is a place
Where my dad says, 'No'
Like the sweet shop

When it's raining
I want to ride my bike
When my mum and dad shout
I want to disappear.

Grace Burnard (7)
Netley Abbey Junior School

Untitled

A theme park is a place
Where I want to feel happy
Like at Hayling Island and in swimming pools

Christmas is a place
Where happy thoughts come back
From many years ago
Like the first Christmas ever!

When it's Christmas I want to feel happy
When it's my birthday
I want to feel proud of myself!

Lilly Hughes (8)
Netley Abbey Junior School

My Cheerful Poem

Cheerful is a place
Where it's noisy and colourful
Like a beautiful rainbow.

Cheerful is a place
Where you can hear birds tweeting
Like music you like listening to.

When it's quiet and dark I want to go to the park
So I can hear people laughing.
When it's nice and colourful
I want to see green, pink, blue, purple and red.

Jessica Parslow (7)
Netley Abbey Junior School

My Tired Poem

Tired is a place
Where it is white, black, grey and brown
Like I am going to fall down a black hole.
When it's white, black, grey and brown
I want to run away to the best place on Earth,

Tired is a place
Where it is frightening and scary
Like you are trapped inside a cloud
When it's frightening and scary
I want to fall to a really happy place.

Sarah Hewlett (7)
Netley Abbey Junior School

My Angry Poem

Angry is a place
A very red place
Like flames in a fire.

Angry is a place
Like lava pouring out of a volcano.

When my face grows red
I just want to punch something.

When it's confusing
I just want to blow.

Lewis Clay (8)
Netley Abbey Junior School

My Sad Poem

Sad is a place, it is very quiet
A room where you can only hear scurrying
When it's quiet all I can hear are fire engines.

Ryan McDonnell (8)
Netley Abbey Junior School

Upset Poem

Upset is a place where
Darkness lays deep and dark
Like in a wood.

Upset is a place
You feel poorly and hurt
Being in a scary hospital for weeks.

When it's dark it makes me upset,
I scream out loud.

When it's dark I hide under the covers.

Sophie Harker (7)
Netley Abbey Junior School

The Cats

Every day they touch me
They always scratch me
Every time they fight
I always cry
They catch mice
Almost twice
When they glare
I get scared
When the cat has a rat
I put it on the doormat.

Jason Leach (10)
Netley Abbey Junior School

My Sad Poem

Sad is a place where it is nice and quiet
You can stay in jail for a week
It's like being on your own
You can sit on your bed to calm down.

Lewis Gale (7)
Netley Abbey Junior School

Night

The night is a trap for anyone who it touches
By the darkness it owns.
At day all you can hear is the children's merriment.
At night the darkness awakes
So does the frightment.
A thought goes through your mind
Of a ghoul taking every soul.
My heart can be dead
Because of the dread.
The night is awake.

Nicole Ojeda Leo (10)
Netley Abbey Junior School

The Devil's Book

The cemetery is the first place to look
For the Devil's evil book.
Only on Hallowe'en will it appear,
But so will the mean men
Following from the rear.
A great friend can Heaven be
But Hell will never be a friend to me.
If the book is ever found,
You will find yourself in Hell,
Then you will really start to yell!

Jack Simmons (10)
Netley Abbey Junior School

My Happy Poem

Happy is a place where it's bright like Paulton's Park.
Unhappy is a place where you're hurt like a graveyard.
When it's bright I want to play with my friends.
When it's hurtful I want to cry out loud.

Bradley Skelton (8)
Netley Abbey Junior School

My Extreme Poem

I feel happy
I feel extreme
I feel like I'm going to scream
The tears from the team
Come from a happy stream.

Ellie-Mae Smith (8)
Netley Abbey Junior School

Deadly Darkness

In the deadly night, comes a white dressing gown
I've never seen before, with no one there.
It's floating by itself.
The stars are in my room with the dressing gown.
I'm so scared, what shall I do?

There the deadly dressing gown stays with one star by its side.
Twinkling while it plays.
My heart is beating like . . . like thunder . . .
It's gone into nothingness.

Courtney Roberts (11)
Netley Abbey Junior School

My Funny Poem

Funny is a place where it is bright and colourful
Like the flames from a fire.

Funny is a place where everyone is laughing
Like a party room.

When it's bright and colourful
Light reaches my eyes, I want to stay there forever.

When it's full of laughter and friends
I want to make 59 friends and come here again tomorrow.

Abigail Bowens (7)
Netley Abbey Junior School

My Lonely Poem

Lonely is a place
Where it's dark and dirty
Like you're trapped in a prison.
Lonely is a place
Where you're on your own like nobody likes you.
When it's all full of cobwebs
And I want to break out and leave
To have a free country
Full of flowers and bad memories have all gone.

Ellie-Mae Lowbridge (7)
Netley Abbey Junior School

Autumn

A stroll on the leaves at the park,
The bright-coloured leaves crackling,
A cold wind is always blowing outside,
A warm heater is always on inside.
At dawn it's freezing,
At dusk it's dark, dark, dark . . . !

Georgia Robinson (10)
Netley Abbey Junior School

My Happy Poem

Happy is a place,
Where it's bright and brilliant.
Happy is a place,
Where it's high and bright
Like up in the sky.
When it's bright and happy
I want to go and have fun.
When it's high and bright
I want to go out to play.

Callum Crotty (7)
Netley Abbey Junior School

The Night Beast

Below the dark night,
The cold blooded beasts lurk,
In search of a snack to satisfy their thirst,
They run like a cheetah out in the wild,
Hoping to extract a weak little child,
They creep up slowly, sneaky and sly,
They capture the child and start to bite.
The sun rises, it's time to leave,
They await in the dungeons till the coming eve.

Daphne Barge (10)
Netley Abbey Junior School

My Upset Poem

Upset is a place
Where darkness lays like the sky at night.
Upset is a place
Where it hurts so much like a scary hospital.
When it's night-time I want to go to bed.
When it's morning I always stay in bed.

Kai Burden (7)
Netley Abbey Junior School

My Upset Poem

Upset is a place
Dark and lonely,
Like in a spooky cave
All on your own.

Upset is a place
Where I'm worried and scared
Like climbing up a tree
Because I might fall.

Molly Moore (7)
Netley Abbey Junior School

My Lonely Poem

Lonely is a place
Where it's dark and deep inside
You feel like someone is following you.

Lonely is a place
Where there's squeaky floorboards
Like there are scary, haunted noises right behind me.

Jake Spanner (7)
Netley Abbey Junior School

Tall Tales

I tell tales, tall, tall tales,
Sometimes they are boring,
Sometimes they are fun.
My friend Margery thinks they are unique,
But my mum thinks they are too neat.
All the teachers at school
Think they are cool,
But my dad thinks they are fools.

Leainya Burden (9)
Netley Abbey Junior School

My Stressed Poem

Stressed is a place
Where it can be big and it can be small
It can be in different places like in your bedroom or school
You just have to leave it alone.
When it's a stressy time it doesn't seem to go
I want to defeat it sometimes.
When it's a stressy time I try to defend myself
I want to catch it in a ball.

Billy Houghton (8)
Netley Abbey Junior School

Untitled

Alisha ate an apple,
The aliens all said, 'Boo!'
The animals were all amazing,
The ants went up to the zoo.
Where are the ants,
The aliens and the mammals?
Hiding with the antelopes!
Can they see you?

Alisha Homer (10)
Netley Abbey Junior School

Untitled

Jacob jumped with
A jelly bean on his jacket
While eating jellyfish.
The jellyfish got a
Jack-in-a-box.
It jumped up and stole his
Jumper while juggling jelly.

Jacob Smith (11)
Netley Abbey Junior School

My Lonely Poem

Lonely is a place
Where it's all dark and damp
Like you are trapped in a cold, dark jail at night
Lonely drips of water come down on your head in a cave
It's dark, you will be scared because there are bats
I want to get out of here
Because I feel better at home with Mum and Dad.

Ellen Mockett (7)
Netley Abbey Junior School

My Happy Poem

Happy is a place
Where the sun shines brightly
Like dolphins leaping high
In the bright blue sky.
When it's the sun shining brightly
I want to swim in Romsey Rapids
Swimming park.

Jay Rowe (7)
Netley Abbey Junior School

My Happy Poem

Happy is a place
Where people dance and play
Like a crazy disco with blaring music
And sparklers hissing
When it's people dancing and playing
I want to dance like a crazy frog.

Nathan Gale (8)
Netley Abbey Junior School

My Sad Poem

Sad is a place
Where dark clouds roam
Like a dark thunderstorm
When there are dark clouds roaming
I want to hide away with the blanket
Over my head where no one can see me.

Ciara Lewis (8)
Netley Abbey Junior School

The Apple Tree

In spring the apple tree blossoms,
Flowers sprout pink and white,
In summer leaves grow,
Petals float down like snow,
And in autumn fruit grows overnight.

Imogen Beesley (10)
Netley Abbey Junior School

My Happy Poem

Florida is a place
Where I like to have lots of fun.
Like going to Disneyland.
When it's very hot
I want to go swimming.

Neil Woodgate (8)
Netley Abbey Junior School

Sad

Sad is a place that people don't like
So those people get so sad
They can't stop thinking about what happened
If they keep thinking about what happened
The person will keep crying lots of times.

Sam Fields (8)
Netley Abbey Junior School

My Tired Poem

Tired is a place
Where it's dark and noisy
Like you're trapped in a roofless flat
When it is dark and noisy
I want to bring someone with me.

Jacob Clothier (7)
Netley Abbey Junior School

My Suspicious Poem

I want to get out of this suspicious place.
Your food would be red and white.
Your clothes are grey and brown.
You would have an orange candle
To light the room up.

Shannon Johnson (7)
Netley Abbey Junior School

My Lonely Poem

Lonely is a place
Where it's dark like you're in prison.
It's like being on your own like nobody likes you.
All you're with is cobwebs and dark shadows.
All of the flowers and memories have gone.

Kayley Carson (7)
Netley Abbey Junior School

My Scary Poem

Scary is a place
Where you are in a dark room all alone
Spooky like a dark cave.
Scary is a place
Where you shiver a lot
Like you are in Antarctica in a snowstorm.
When it's scary time
I want to snuggle up in a quilt
When it's dark and worrying
Go somewhere bright and sunny.

Reece Griffiths (8)
Netley Abbey Junior School

My Lonely Poem

Lonely is a place
Where it's a quiet, dark cave
Like a gloomy, damp, scary cave
Where it's a scary, boring cave with lots of monsters
Like a spooky cave with lots of puddles
When it's quiet and dark and lots of shadows
I want to take a friend to keep me company
When it's quiet and dark you can't see a thing
I want to be brave and go in by myself.

Jayden Davies (7)
Netley Abbey Junior School

My Senses

When I touch my cat's fur
She likes to purr.
It's something I like to hear
It's music to my ear.
When I touch my cat's tail
I get delivered mail.
When I eat my food
I'm in a good mood.
When I eat my fish
I lick my lips.
My favourite smell is Marmite
It smells just right.
When I smell my dinner
I think I'm getting slimmer.
I really like to see my nan
I'm her number one fan.
When I see my mum
My homework gets done.

James Clarke (9)
St Luke's CE Primary School, Sway

Love

Love feels like a bubble in the air with a red fluffy loveheart
inside with people kissing.
Love sounds as sweet as two people looking at each other
for evermore in a massive bubble in the sky.
Love tastes like a lovely candy bar in a shop full of sweets
as sweet as a pack of red roses.
Love smells like a rose-scented candle in the centre
of your heart.
Love is the most gorgeous couple to be made for now
and for evermore.
Love reminds me of a happy family playing in the park,
also having lots of fun.

Suzy Judd
St Luke's CE Primary School, Sway

Love!

Love tastes like ice cream with a topping of strawberries,
marshmallows and chocolate all put together.
Love feels like everlasting happiness like being on a cruise
on the ocean of sparkly love, calm and with dolphins jumping
in and out of the sea and that is what it feels like.
Love is as red as roses blossoming in my heart.
Love is red like sweet plumped red lips on Christmas Day.
Love reminds me of Easter, roses, hearts, delicious chocolate
brownies, dolphins jumping in and out of the sparkly, shiny,
spine-tingling water.
Also bright gleaming light twinkling in the bright sunny sky.
Love sounds like birds cheeping in the wind and breeze.
Also sounds like the rainforest and the waves swaying
side to side.
Love looks like big fluffy clouds in the sky,
also doves flying with joy and excitement.
It's amazing how many words are in love.

Jasmine Roberts
St Luke's CE Primary School, Sway

Love

Love is a great emotion that everyone has.
It is a smile on someone's face.
Love is a glowing sun, bringing light and joy to the world.
Love tastes like a sugary sweet dancing on my tongue.
Love is a big red heart that makes people happy.
Love feels like a big fluffy cushion, sunlight on your cheeks.
Love reminds me of a big cheesy grin, planted on my face.
Love sounds like the beating of wings
as geese fly through the sunlit sky.
Love is my family, my friends and my dog.
Love is my home, my school and my hobbies.
Love smells like melted chocolate pouring from the pan.
Love is a great emotion that everybody has!

Racheal Brangan (10)
St Luke's CE Primary School, Sway

Love

Love reminds you of a first kiss, a first true relationship,
the one you have always loved.
Love is what you want it to be and will dwell
in your heart forever.
Love tastes like minty gum, never losing its taste,
chocolate melting in your mouth
or it can be like a broken heart, as sour as one million
fizzy sweets stuffed in your mouth.
Love looks like a field of sunflowers glimmering in the sun.
Love is pink, red, blue, it is happy colours.
Love feels like a hug given by the fluffy clouds of Heaven.
Love smells of lavender, lavender blossoming
in an enchanted garden.
Love sounds like the birds tweeting, the never-ending
beating of a true relationship.
It's amazing that all these things can be put into one word - love.

Fraser Owen (11)
St Luke's CE Primary School, Sway

Bravery

Bravery's colour is black and dull because you could be
using bravery like no one else can.
Bravery tastes like a flavour sensation in your mouth exploding
with greatness because you are knowing everyone knows
about your great bravery.
Bravery looks like men, women and children cheering you on
with smiles on their faces.
Bravery smells of great smells like chocolate truffles
and maybe not so great things like sweat.
Bravery feels like many people patting you on the back
giving you glory and respect.
Bravery sounds like people screaming your name
with many smiles and sparkling eyes.

Robbie Stafford (10)
St Luke's CE Primary School, Sway

Fear

Fear looks like when you shiver and cover up into a corner
and you stare at the window when you can't get to sleep.
When you shiver to death over a fright of someone
jumping out at you at midnight.
A girl screaming out at midnight, waking an old body up
from the zombie yard.
A fear of tasting so fat, so horrible, so hard, so oily,
so old, so grim!
It reminds me of the first time I went on my mini moto.
I tested it out in my back garden.
I went forward and did a wheelie.
A man walked in front of me
and I accidentally hit him in the privates - *ouch!*
The colour of the mini moto was blue, white, red
but now it's black and red.

Ryan Jones (10)
St Luke's CE Primary School, Sway

Love

Love - it feels like you're floating on lovely sunset clouds
which are pink in the lovely light, you're just floating along.
Love is lots of colours but mostly gold, this gold is as golden
as the sun glistening down on the happy couple glowing
at each other with hearts, golden hearts,
in their eyes glinting in the light.
Love is the smell of the flowers in the garden or the fruit,
like reddening apples and gorgeous green pears.
Love is everywhere.
The flowers go into the perfume and it now is sprinkling down.
Love looks like the children running around having fun.
Love is lovely, it's the people's beating hearts.

Maisie Ovenden
St Luke's CE Primary School, Sway

Pride

The colour of pride is green for go and the colour of grass swaying, silence in cold breeze.
Pride feels strong also happy, wonderful to feel just like running in a beautiful meadow of daisies, tweeting birds above you.
Pride sounds like two hummingbirds getting pollen out of colourful sweet-smelling honeysuckle.
Pride smells of a vanilla and chocolate scented candle burning in the dark.
Pride tastes like chocolate melting in your mouth.
Pride reminds you of winning a race and being the champion and a round of applause just for you.
Pride looks like a pile of gold and money.

Samantha Claven
St Luke's CE Primary School, Sway

Fear

Fear feels like a lump of emotion in your stomach
that is weighing you down.
Fear sounds like your heart is thumping against your ribcage with the intensity of a lion watching its prey.
Fear smells of carrion rotting with ravens pecking at it.
Fear tastes like a raw and bitter berry that
you can't digest easily.
It reminds me of being rooted to the spot with anxiety
flowing through me.
Fear looks like the dark hours with no hope.
Fear is the most miserable colour anyone could dream up because of its overwhelming feeling.

Craig Dearnley
St Luke's CE Primary School, Sway

Pride

Pride reminds me of a warm glowing sun in America
in a swimming pool.
Pride tastes like a chocolate fountain with fluffy,
sticky cooked marshmallows.
Pride smells of vanilla essence with added highlights
of strawberry and chocolate.
Sad and disappointment for others.
Pride sounds like bravery and a whistle blowing in your heart.
Pride is as yellow as the warm glow of a burning sun.
Pride feels like your heart swelling up with a flower blooming
in your ever-growing, ever-beating heart.

Lauren Stevens
St Luke's CE Primary School, Sway

Love

Love sounds like a baby blue tit that has just come out
of its egg and has just discovered a new world.
Love looks like a phenomenal sunset just rising.
Love smells like a mouthwatering, heart thumping,
Cadbury's chocolate bar.
Love tastes like a staggering strawberry with melted chocolate on.
The colour of love is the bright orange of the breathtaking sun.
Love reminds me of a baby deer taking its first steps
of the amazing world.
Love feels like you have just broken the world record
of a tennis grand slam!

Joseph Lewis (10)
St Luke's CE Primary School, Sway

Fear

Fear looks like a lonely candle, sat shaking as well as burning
in the dark midnight sky.
Fear reminds me of a cold heart as black as ink,
screaming for help.
It tastes cold, mouldy and scared.
Fear smells of death, anything but love.
The colour of fear is grey like old men's hair
And black like sorrow.
Fear feels cold like the Atlantic or a poem without happiness.
Fear sounds like a little boy sat in the street with his heart
pounding because of his chest's cold.

Georgia King (10)
St Luke's CE Primary School, Sway

Pride

Pride looks like passion.
Pride is a bright, beautiful colour.
Pride sounds like an extra loud applause from all your beloved.
Pride reminds me of managing to get 19 out of 20
in my mind-boggling maths test.
Pride smells of when you've just finished cooking your best barbecue
ever (hopefully with no burnt sausages!)
Pride feels like a proud parent after they've just finished
reading a great report.
Pride tastes of sweetness.

Amy Hilton
St Luke's CE Primary School, Sway

Sadness

Sadness looks like a shaking red face, scared to the bone.
Sadness tastes like a salt-filled ocean filling an empty ditch.
Sadness smells of salty tears rolling down a forgotten face.
Sadness feels like icy cold footballs hitting you on the back every second of darkness.
Sadness reminds me of the day my dad left me.
Sadness is the colour of an icy dart, striking a broken heart.
The colour of blue salty water dripping down a tired red face.
Sadness is a missing link to a happy family.

Grace Halligan (10)
St Luke's CE Primary School, Sway

Sadness

Sadness smells of the horrors of death and nightmares.
Sadness sounds like the shriek of the dead.
Sadness is like an arrow of death
going through the unsuspecting body.
Sadness smells of rotting roses in the winter.
Sadness looks like the corpse of a great deer.
Sadness tastes like a bitter poison.
Sadness feels like a porcupine on sulphur.
Sadness is black as a puma.

Billy Beeson (10)
St Luke's CE Primary School, Sway

Love

Love feels like a candle, lit in darkness on a calming day.
Love is as red as a bright rose sweeping across my soul.
Delicious strawberry chocolate sweeping across my mind.
Love looks like a great romance in the air.
Love reminds me of a baby donkey
walking across the beautiful road.

Jake Spooner (10)
St Luke's CE Primary School, Sway

Pride

Pride feels like a bride with the groom.
Pride smells like dried hair after a swimming race.
Pride reminds me of the class assembly about food.
Pride looks like a round of applause.
Pride tastes like glory.
Pride's colour is red and yellow, even orange.
Pride looks like happiness in your eyes, twinkling with pride.
Pride sounds like sweat dripping down your cheek.
Pride is lots of things!

Jake Pritchard (9)
St Luke's CE Primary School, Sway

Fear

Fear sounds like a flower closing its delicate petals,
getting ready for the long damp night ahead of it.
Fear tastes like a sour mint sizzling in the everlasting
heat of a dry mouth.
Fear reminds me of a lonely heart sitting in a cold chest.
Fear looks like a grey bubble floating in a river of tears.
Fear is the colour of the blackest rain cloud in the sky.
Fear feels like a lump of emotions in a pit of sadness.

Natasha Gibbs
St Luke's CE Primary School, Sway

Sadness

Sadness is as blue as the Atlantic Ocean.
Sadness is the taste of a bitter orange.
Sadness looks like an upset heart.
Sadness smells like a lost bunny rabbit searching for his mum.
Sadness reminds me of my pet cat that has died.
Sadness sounds like a lost child crying.
Sadness feels like a broken heart.

Amy Thompson
St Luke's CE Primary School, Sway

Joy

Joy tastes like milk chocolate melting in your mouth.
Joy looks like happiness in a very big park.
Joy feels like kind people lifting you up to the heavens.
Joy sounds like people having fun in a secondary school.
Joy smells of lavender and roses
mixed with the marvellous poppies.
Joy reminds me of coming 3rd or 4th in a football tournament.
Joy is the colour of yellow and the hot sun burning on the sand.

Charlie Weekes
St Luke's CE Primary School, Sway

Silence

Silence is as quiet as a leaf falling from its broad tree.
Silence looks like a soft, fluffy cloud floating in the moonlight.
Silence smells of spectacular spices wafting
like a bird high in the sky.
Silence is the colour of water trickling down your arm.
Silence looks like a solemn tree waving in the autumn wind.
Silence is the sound of soft wintry rain pattering on the doorstep.
Silence tastes of victory floating in the cold night air.

Helena Beachey-Tendyra (9)
St Luke's CE Primary School, Sway

Fun

Fun tastes like chocolate floating across a beautiful slow
running sea.
Fun looks like people playing happily in the sunset.
The colour of fun is light blue like the lovely clouds.
Fun feels like enjoyment, a happy feeling inside all of you.
Fun smells of happiness and friendship and lavender.
Fun reminds me of my friends and me playing happily with them.
Fun sounds like people laughing, talking and enjoying themselves.

Charlotte Pugh
St Luke's CE Primary School, Sway

Silence

Silence is like a candle burning brightly in a dark room.
Silence sounds like the wind drifting by like a dash of lightning.
Silence reminds me of a sleeping cat on a window sill.
Silence feels like a ghost talking to me.
Silence smells like sunflowers in the sunshine.
Silence looks like a bird flying high.
Silence tastes of a tasty strawberry cheesecake.

Tazmin Toms (10)
St Luke's CE Primary School, Sway

Love

Love is the colour of red blossom in a magnificent garden.
Love smells of roses and chocolate mixed together.
Love looks like a red rose floating in the air.
Love feels like you're in a warm sauna dwelling there for eternity.
Love sounds like beautiful birds chirping at sunrise.
Love tastes like the sweet, melting honey.
Love reminds me of a joyful family or couple.

Sam Morgan (10)
St Luke's CE Primary School, Sway

Love

Love is the wonderful colours of red and pink.
Love smells like a lovely, sizzling sausage.
Love sounds like a frying pan cooking a pancake.
Love feels like a loveable love film.
Love looks like an attractive person.
Love reminds people of good and bad times.
Love tastes of lovehearts.

Charlotte Elford (9)
St Luke's CE Primary School, Sway

Silence

Silence is as black as a jaguar hunting its prey.
Silence feels like blankness just sat in the winter air.
Silence smells like a damp snowy night.
Silence reminds me of ghosts and all things bad.
Silence tastes of sticky maple syrup.
Silence looks like a cold misty morning.
Silence sounds like silence.

Lucy Moxom (11)
St Luke's CE Primary School, Sway

Love

Love sounds like a sound you love.
Love reminds me of my family that I love.
Love is as red as a heart, pink as a pink flower swaying in the wind.
Love is when you get that very first kiss.
Love smells like a box of chocolates sent by your loved ones.
Love is the taste of chocolate given to you on Valentine's Day.
Love looks like hearts over a lovely couple.

Leah Gill
St Luke's CE Primary School, Sway

Pride

Pride smells of the victory that a lucky person has had.
It smells like happiness mixed in with roses of the garden in Heaven.
Pride tastes like the sweet sugar of a cake oozing with cream.
Pride is the colour of blue when you are swimming
in the water of everlasting life.
Pride feels like a fluffy ball of happiness floating like a feather
that you could dwell on forever.

Lewis Reeves
St Luke's CE Primary School, Sway

Fun

Fun sounds like children playing and running
in the burning sun.
Fun feels like you're in charge of your own world
where no one else is.
Fun reminds me of football after school with my friend.
Fun is the colour white for the children playing
under the fluffy clouds.

Luke Lewis (11)
St Luke's CE Primary School, Sway

Bravery

Bravery is an enormous lion eating a snake with a venomy sting.
The colour of bravery is red for the blood pumping fast which will
dwell in your body forever.
It smells of pride and really nice deodorant.
It reminds me of war, blood and lots of bones.
It tastes of sweat and blood.
It sounds like shouting and gun powder.

James Mantle (10)
St Luke's CE Primary School, Sway

Happiness

Happiness feels like soft pillows and marshmallows,
Happiness smells like violets on a summer's day,
Happiness reminds me of when I last received
a certificate in assembly.
Happiness sounds like laughing and cheering,
Happiness tastes of the sweetest oranges grown in Britain,
Happiness is the best feeling in the world!

Daniel Stone
St Luke's CE Primary School, Sway

Bravery!

Bravery reminds me of reaching the top of the rock wall.
Bravery's colour is orange because it's not exactly angry.
Bravery smells like a long, never-ending hall full of sweat.
Bravery feels as though you've just been scared
and have a lump in your neck.
Bravery sounds like a furious heart pounding.
Bravery looks like life.

Oliver Boyland
St Luke's CE Primary School, Sway

Fear

Fear is white, as white as the snow on top of the highest mountain.
Fear looks like you have seen an ugly monster say hello to you.
Fear sounds like a ghostly wail inside you.
Fear feels like a cold shiver down your back.
Fear tastes like bitter dough.
Fear is not nice.

Natasha Hall
St Luke's CE Primary School, Sway

Untitled

Sadness is a dull colour.
Sadness feels scary.
Sadness is like being lonely.
Sadness sounds like windy air.
Sadness smells like mould across food.
Sadness tastes like smelly, stinky chips.

Ryan Pope
St Luke's CE Primary School, Sway

Silence

Silence is a beautiful land that is yet to be discovered,
Silence smells like a damp dungeon far, far away,
Silence sounds like a dragonfly fluttering round a lake,
Silence feels like dread bubbling up inside you,
Silence is a white seagull flying over the ocean,
Silence tastes like pure water flowing down a stream.

Katie Lenton
St Luke's CE Primary School, Sway

Silence

Silence sounds like peaceful wind blowing in the trees.
Silence tastes like a scrumptious dinner in a posh café.
Silence smells like a bunch of lovely roses.
Silence looks like the lovely, refreshing blue sky.
Silence feels like a fluffy, bouncy cushion.
Silence reminds me of a peaceful library with silence all around.

Jamie Ellis (10)
St Luke's CE Primary School, Sway

Silence

Silence is when your closed mouth does not speak at all.
Silence is when the air is cold and ice-cold.
Silence feels like you're the only one in the world.
Silence smells like your mum's baking cakes from the kitchen.
Silence reminds me of when I had a dare to be quiet for an hour.
Silence sounds like children having fun with their friends.

Lauren Bailey
St Luke's CE Primary School, Sway

Pride

Pride tastes like fish and chips.
Pride is beautiful bright blue.
Pride feels like an impressed parent at our assembly.
Pride smells of a brightly-coloured candle on a dark, gloomy night.
Pride sounds like the tide at a sunny beach.
Pride is happiness and excitement in your ear.

Kira Marsh
St Luke's CE Primary School, Sway

Bravery

The colour of bravery is ruby-red and dangerous.
Bravery tastes like warm confidence sizzling in my tummy.
Bravery reminds me of Rin Tin Tin, the bravest dog ever.
Bravery smells like a hot dog sizzling and rumbling in the oven.
Bravery feels like proud, furry animals' fur, nice, warm and fuzzy.
Bravery sounds like a confident person.

Issy Cryer
St Luke's CE Primary School, Sway

Bravery

Bravery reminds me of when I overcame my fear
of the midnight darkness.
Bravery feels like you have grown massive muscles in your arms.
Bravery is the colour cotton-white, the colour you love.
Bravery smells like a sweet smell of victory.
Bravery tastes like crunchy chicken dippers.

Bethan Keen
St Luke's CE Primary School, Sway

Joy

Joy tastes like a hot chocolate with oozing marshmallows.
It reminds me of the first space shuttle launch into space.
It looks like happy children in a playground having a good time.
It sounds like an old rusty car that's just started.
It is the colour of joy which is a hot oven that comes from the sun.

Luke Green
St Luke's CE Primary School, Sway

Silence

Silence is the classroom.
Silence sounds like a deserted building.
Silence looks like dull colours and closed mouths.
Silence tastes like water, purer than our bodies.
Silence feels different at times.

Tom Clover (9)
St Luke's CE Primary School, Sway

Fun

Fun tastes like sour sweets fizzing in my mouth.
Fun feels like a tingle down your spine.
Fun reminds you of a sensational time you had yesterday.
Fun sounds like everybody's having a lovely time.
Fun is a very bright yellow.

Jos Whitehorn (10)
St Luke's CE Primary School, Sway

Happiness

Happiness feels like a dream sent from Heaven, up above.
Happiness smells like a bunch of cherries ready to be picked.
Happiness reminds me of families celebrating on Christmas Day.
Happiness sounds like a bunch of people laughing.

Ryan Drayton
St Luke's CE Primary School, Sway

The Magic Box
(Based on ' Magic Box' by Kit Wright)

I will put into the box . . .
The silver saliva of a silk dragon,
The wick of a wizard's wondrous wand waiting to cast
a cursed enchantment on the innocent enemy,
Scarlet-red blood glistening on the top of a vampire's fang.

I will put into the box . . .
A mystical monkey shooting through the sky on a shimmering
star, passing the mysterious midnight moon, illuminated
by a myriad of golden suns,
Lewis Hamilton riding a ten tonne woolly mammoth
and an ancient caveman driving a Formula One,
The swishing sound of the silvery salty sea slashing
on the sandy rocks.
The first ray of sunshine in the midst of creation,
The bite of a king cobra oozing with venom.

My box is fashioned from bloodstained silver, glimmering gold
and dazzling diamond,
With snowflakes on the lid and curses in the corners,
Its hinges are the claws of a scorpion.

I shall parachute in my box over the vivid rainbow
that brings colour to the sky,
Then land on an undiscovered island.

Daniel Chapero-Hall (10)
St Swithun's Primary School, Portsmouth

The Magic Box
(Based on 'Magic Box' by Kit Wright)

I will put in my box . . .
An exquisite shell from a sacred cave hidden in the depths
of the shimmering sea,
A flash of light flickering through an ancient magic book
turning the pages rapidly,
A rhythmic beat racing through the air against the strong wind.

I will put in my box . . .
A brown elephant galloping through the perfect view
of the countryside with its hair following behind
and a grey horse plodding clumsily through the dusty roads
of Africa,
The sound of a newborn baby laughing with a tremendous
smile and a great grandma coming to her old age,
remembering all the wondrous memories
of being a young child,
The sound of birds cheeping away like mad, through the radiant
spring and autumn leaves rustling across the frozen ground.

I will put in my box . . .
The heart and thought of a river flowing to the cool still water
of Lake Valchime,
The colours of the last rainbow there was, swirling in the fantasy
of my dreams,
A bouncy ball rolling to my dreamy desires of happiness.

I will put in my box . . .
Sudden movement of a hyena moving across the jungle,
darting through the trees,
A thunder clap lasting 11 seconds precisely, saved from a rapid
windy storm,
A glistening, clinquant, glossy diamond found from a very high
reaching mountain inside the crumbly rocks.

In my magic box I would scuba dive, looking for diamonds,
shells and so many more things.
Also I would have that totally cool feeling with water rushing
through my silky hair and being so free,
seeing all the colourful fish!

Isabel Thompson-Whiteside (9)
St Swithun's Primary School, Portsmouth

The Magic Box
(Based on 'Magic Box' by Kit Wright)

I will put in the box . . .
a big, black, grizzly bear with a rumbly tummy
a big, fuzzy snowman with a heart of stone
a fluffy candyfloss cloud.

I will put in the box . . .
a sea with sparkly shells
a gentle breeze on a summer's day
a dolphin with sharp, bloody fangs.

I will put in the box . . .
a white, pearly dove with golden wings
a tree with rainbow lollipops
a bone of a dinosaur.

My box is fashioned from metal, gold and silver
with dogs on the lid and wolves in the corners.
Its hinges are the toe joints of rabbits.

I shall ride in a motorboat on the most pearly blue seas
and then ride ashore on a stony beach.

Aleksandra Ruzik (9)
St Swithun's Primary School, Portsmouth

I Want To Paint

I want to paint a glimmering fairy standing proud
on a Christmas tree
I want to paint the cluck of a rooster waking you up
in the morning from a deep sleep
I want to paint a newborn puppy opening his big blue
bulging eyes and curling into a ball
I want to paint the taste of a juicy strawberry
dipped in chocolate
I want to paint the smell of a blown out candle
melting from the heat
I want to paint a sneezing snake suffering from 'Swine Flu'
I want to paint a pony with rosy lips strutting down a field,
like a model down a catwalk
I want to paint the view of space with all the stars gleaming
in front of me
But I can't find my paintbrush!

Helena Cox-Smith (10)
St Swithun's Primary School, Portsmouth

I Want To Paint . . .

I want to paint a rainbow fish diving in and out
of the baby blue sea.
I want to paint a sugar cube slowly dissolving
on the tip of a tongue.
I want to paint a 16-week-old rabbit taking its first joyful hops.
I want to paint a flat on fire, oozing out its sneaking, strong
smoke into coughing people's lungs.
I want to paint the bottom of the sea full of gold
from the sunken ships.
I want to paint a limo speeding to its next stop
before it gets a complaint.
I want to paint a polka dot horse galloping to victory.
But now I am out of ideas!

Francesca Furtado Mills (10)
St Swithun's Primary School, Portsmouth

I Want To Paint

I want to paint the love and affection of a newborn kitten
as it purrs around the legs of its mother.
I want to paint the heart of a guide dog as it leads its owner
around the hazards of the city.
I want to paint the fragile flame of a flickering candle
as it fights to stay alight.
I want to paint the sigh of relief as the first puppy of the litter
opens its bulging eyes and looks longingly at its mother.
I want to paint the sound of children singing in assemblies
as I walk through the corridor.
I want to paint the little old lady who lives in the shoe.
I want to paint the first leaf that the very hungry caterpillar
took a bite out of.
Well that would be nice but remember we are in reality
and I would need to see the little old lady who lived in a shoe
to paint her.

India Beaumont (10)
St Swithun's Primary School, Portsmouth

I Want To Paint

I want to paint a cool caterpillar chewing cauliflower.
I want to paint a busy bumblebee stinging an old lady's bottom.
I want to paint a zebra with a long trunk and floppy grey ears
and an elephant with hooves and black and white stripes.
I want to paint the taste of giggling gooseberries,
bubbling blueberries and silly strawberries
bouncing around in my tummy.
I want to paint a flying pig in space, eating sugar cubes
and mini cupcakes and drinking tea with a purple tabby cat.
I want to paint a blue flamingo, tap dancing on a fluffy cloud
of candyfloss.
But I have no paint!

Gaia Osborne (9)
St Swithun's Primary School, Portsmouth

I Want To Paint

I want to paint a baby dolphin being born
I want to paint a sherbet sweet making my mouth watery
I want to paint an orange Ferrari that goes as fast as a cheetah
Hunting down his buffalo
I want to paint a glimmering sea as calm as a baby sleeping
I want to paint a smiling crocodile swimming around the River Nile
I want to paint a talking tiger telling a woman to run
I want to paint a flying dog taking a child to their beautiful dreams
I want to paint a 1000-year-old ghost tap dancing
I want to paint a fat red elephant doing ballet
I want to paint a shiny green alien with one eye
Who is partying all night.

Freya Temple (10)
St Swithun's Primary School, Portsmouth

I Want To Paint

I want to paint a roasted marshmallow on a BBQ
I want to paint a cow on a racetrack running fast
I want to paint the Stig driving a limo at top speed
I want to paint melted chocolate mixed with apple,
melted up into slices
I want to paint a beautiful flower eating grass
I want to paint a can with a tutu and worse, it is bright pink
I want to paint a day on a surfboard
Sorry, I have to dash.

Sophie Carabott (9)
St Swithun's Primary School, Portsmouth

I Want To Paint

I want to paint marshmallows dipped in melted white chocolate.
I want to paint a tap dancing tiny tulip.
I want to paint three little kittens cuddling up to me.
I want to paint ants ice skating on an ice cube.
I want to paint an old car starting its engine like a train.
'Oh no I've just remembered, I've got to go to school, must dash!'

Patrick Carden (9)
St Swithun's Primary School, Portsmouth

Do Not Stand By My Grave And Weep
(Inspired by 'Do Not Stand At My Grave And Weep' by Mary Frye)

Do not stand by my grave and weep
I am not there, I do not sleep

I am the leaf that did not die
I am the warm summer sky
I am the love filling the air
I am the tree, cold and bare

I am the wind howling at night
I am the bird in mid-flight
I am the cat in your arms
I am the crisp hay in the barns

I am the surprise in the Christmas box
I am the stray hunting fox
I am the wheat on the farm
I am the wind, small but calm

Do not stand by my grave and weep
I am not there, I do not sleep
Do not stand by my grave and cry
I am not there, I did not die.

Daniel Coleman (10)
Stoke Park Junior School

Bombed

The war started, Hitler made his first bomb,
All you could hear was bricks falling, people screaming,
All you could see was people sleeping in a river of blood.

Hilter came to bomb again but we were prepared,
There were not as many people sleeping in blood,
Not as many bricks falling.

But there were more people screaming,
The air raid sirens went off for the first time,
The spotlights were used for the first time.

Everyone rushed to the shelters,
The bombs fell like rain.

The war finished.
We won,
There were no more people sleeping in rivers of blood,
No more bricks falling,
No more screaming.

Tyler Kowalewicz (10)
Stoke Park Junior School

Two Voices

As sinking ships fall under, new ships are rising.
The sound of young children crying to their mothers fills
the street as young children sing happily.
Blood fields fill the country, beautiful poppies grow strong
through the dry rubble.
Bombs falling like the cold winter snow but children play
with a bouncy ball on the wrecked street.
Bricks falling to the ground as helpless bodies lay
on their warm beds.
Gunshots fill the misty sky as the rain drips onto a spring leaf.
As sirens make people scatter to safety, a mother cradles
her baby with a lullaby.

Lucy Spake (10)
Stoke Park Junior School

Two Voices

As the air raid passes there are joyful owls hooting
in the misty moonlight.
The sound of sirens screaming to the world, as joyful owls
glide through the misty sky.
Poisonous gases are invading the air, as children and parents
make the happiness last.
Evacuated children cry while the other teenagers
are left all alone.
Bombs are fired in the blue gloomy air,
the bombs are like floating balloons in the moonlight.
Lying dead on the floor, no blood running, it's Sergeant.
It is too late, he has gone,
although he has died in an amazing poppy field.
As gunpowder is shot through the air, it feels as though
it is red-blooded poppies flowing through the sky . . .
Demolished, our world is all wrecked to bits.

Maddie Lewis (10)
Stoke Park Junior School

Two Voices

As the air raid rages during the night, the owls start gliding
during their flight as a siren sounds.
When the bullets shatter on the rooftops, the heavy rain
thumps the roofs of houses.
As you can hear a crying mother cry, her son wishes
that her tears were meant to be happy.
The smell of gas warns the men it's nearby and an adult fills
up a swimming pool on a hot summer's day.
A flash in the distance is like lots of candles being lit
on a Hallowe'en night.
Now the baby has fallen asleep from a lullaby as loads
of bombs are being dropped on the city of London.
Now the men are asleep having peace and in our minds
they are still alive.

Kieran Sheppard-Laing (10)
Stoke Park Junior School

I Am King!

My name is Lion and I am king . . . my teeth are
staggering swords
My name is Lion and I am king . . . I have a large mane
for showing off
My name is Lion and I am king . . . my razor-sharp claws
are like mounted penknives
My name is Lion and I am king . . . my startling jaw
is as powerful as a wrestler
My name is Lion and I am king . . . my swift legs
are as fast as a shark
My name is Lion and I am king . . . my cubs are
as cute as a puppy
My name is Lion and I am king . . . I am as mean as a devil
My name is Lion and I am king . . . and if you don't stay away
I will get you!

Joshua Moore (9)
Stoke Park Junior School

Two Voices

As soldiers softly weep in their beds,
there are men lying in their hospital beds thankful for their lives.
Sometimes there are wives ignoring the pain of the loss
of their loved ones,
where on the other hand there are ladies in their gardens
proud for their relatives as the breeze hits their faces.
You also hear the heavy bangs of the bodies crashing
to the ground as the war carries on,
where there are many sweet sounds of the birds humming
sounds as they glide through the gentle breeze.
There are also rough sounds coming through the ground
as the children get dragged away from their families,
as they make their way to the evacuation train,
as the horn goes off on the train they wave goodbye.

Jack Ryves (10)
Stoke Park Junior School

Two Voices

The houses that have been crushed by falling bombs
as the light rain on the rooftops helps the boy fall to sleep.
The sound of people screaming everywhere you go
as the sound of birds humming in the green trees.
The sight of people dying on a dark and weak day,
the sight of people walking by the fresh apple trees.
The smell of fire and gas, the smell of sweet hot chocolate.
The feel of broken toys and smashed up bricks,
the feel of fresh clear water.
The sound of children crying, the sound of children playing
with each other by the fresh green grass.

Max Pitman (11)
Stoke Park Junior School

Two Voices In The Air

Worn out soldiers trapped in the iron ship but nothing other
than helpless tuna who scrabble caught in the net.
A mother lies in a never-ending sleep on the grass as a deer
lies in a soft dreamy sleep.
Clouds of CS gas suffocate people below but it's only birds
gathering to sing a song.
The sound of sirens make people flee to shelters as joyful owls
glide in the fluffy clouds.
Horses are spooked from the sound of gunshots
but it's nothing other than them enjoying a race around
the poppy field.

Jasmine Sims (10)
Stoke Park Junior School

Untitled

It was so peaceful that I heard . . . a pencil slowly rotting away
to catch the pen.
It was so silent that I heard . . . my next door neighbour
gulping her drink.
It was so calm that I heard . . . a pink pencil nagging a ruler
if it could walk across it.
It was so quiet that I heard . . . a baby crying to get some
attention from its mum.
It was so still that I heard . . . a bin munching
the Chinese food in it.

Oliver Wright (7)
Stoke Park Junior School

The Rhino

I am the rhino broad and strong
I am the rhino trudging along
I am the rhino old but bold
I am the rhino who is not told
I am the rhino who rolls in the mud
I am the rhino who would give you a thud
I am the rhino who has horns like thorns
I am the rhino with rough, tough skin
I am the rhino, that is my name,
playing strong, that is my game.

Louie Meleder (9)
Stoke Park Junior School

I Am The Leopard

I am the leopard who is as vicious as can be.
I am the leopard with pure white whiskers.
I am the leopard with eyes that gleam like diamonds.
I am the leopard with the strongest, wealthiest body.

Tasmin Smith (9)
Stoke Park Junior School

The Rhino

I am the rhino who has skin as rough as bark.
I am the rhino who hides from the dark.
I am the beast who has a mighty horn.
I am the rhino who wakes at dawn.
I am the rhino who eats all day.
I am the rhino who likes the month of May.
I am the rhino who has black eyes.
I am the rhino who is as big as a tree.
I am the rhino who likes to roam free.
I am the rhino who's better than the rest!

Ben Sutcliffe (9)
Stoke Park Junior School

I Am A Lion

I am a lion, my mane is as bouncy as a ball of wool.
I am a lion, my teeth are as sharp as a razor-sharp dagger.
I am a lion, my fur is like a doormat
that has been used 100 times.
I am a lion, my eyes are like big, glowing, shiny marbles.
I am a lion, my nose is as dark as coal.
I am a lion, my ears are like huge roses.
I am a lion, my tail is as bendy as a piece of rope.
I am a lion, I have paws as powerful as a motorbike.

Simon Hancock (9)
Stoke Park Junior School

I Am The Cheetah

I am the cheetah with spots as dark as the midnight sky.
I am the cheetah as fast as lightning and never shy.
I am the cheetah with black eyes as spooky as a misty pond.
I am the cheetah with ears like mountains and as dark as caves.
I am the cheetah with a nose as black as a zebra's stripes.

Elizabeth Earl (9)
Stoke Park Junior School

Two Voices

As the air raids are rushing through the darkness,
there is no sound beneath the moonlight.
As I hear the horrible sounds of a woman crying
from near and far,
the owls are hooting high up in the treetops.
The guns are firing like rockets, therefore the guns
are clicking with all the ammunition used up.
The bodies are resting from being shattered to pieces
as the soldiers are snoring in their beds.

Lewis Pople (10)
Stoke Park Junior School

Two Voices

Someone got shot in the pumping, red, warm heart,
as you can feel your cheerful life running through your body.
When the weeping mother says goodbye
to her evacuated children, the choir sings.
As the deadly bombs drop suddenly through
the wonderful blue sky.
The flash bang guns, like the campfire is sparking up.
The air raid sirens go off, whilst the joyful owl's hooting
in the moonlight.

Jack Lawrence (10)
Stoke Park Junior School

I Am A Lion

I am a lion with my golden yellow coat under the glimmering sun
Slyly I pounce towards my predators
I roar as loud as a radio at the highest amount of volume
I am a lion with my beautiful orange mane
I am racing the wind
I am a lion.

Alice Wilmot (9)
Stoke Park Junior School

Two Voices

The sounds of the air raid sirens in the air,
owls hooting along to it too.
The shouting voices of men but faith of them all.
The bombs like fireworks crashing in the night sky.
The firing of guns, wild and free, swiping bullets through the air.
The sounds of the sirens, many planes
but as the owl glides in the thunderous sky.
Two men shouting but forgiving of them all.
The army lost on the battlefield but it's hopeful for them all.

Ben Vincent (10)
Stoke Park Junior School

I Am The Cheetah

I am the cheetah, my spots are as black as a dark cave.
I am the cheetah, my fur is as gentle as cotton wool.
I am the cheetah, my nose is as wet as the deep blue sea.
I am the cheetah, my ears are as cute and cuddly as a soft cloud.
I am the cheetah with very small claws.
I am the cheetah with powerful legs.
I am the cheetah with bones as strong as a sumo wrestler.
I am the cheetah with the spiky hair.
I am the cheetah with claws as sharp as a pin.

James Beadle (9)
Stoke Park Junior School

Two Voices

As the men fell one by one,
it was like blossom falling off the trees in the countryside.
As death cries screamed one at a time,
I heard the sound of victory in the city.
As friends die right in front of you,
as children are born right in front of you.

Daniel Whitehead (10)
Stoke Park Junior School

Two Voices

The bullet that smashed into a man's flesh,
as a bird flew close to him.
As a man is screaming help and as a bird is calling
for its babies to come back.
Bombs falling like lightning strikes, as birds dive from the sky.
Blood on every man, water on every baby.
Planes falling from the sky as a skydiver diving from a plane.
Guns firing in the distance and as birds fly in the distance.
Buildings falling from a bomb, birds falling from a tree.

Jamie Cattle (10)
Stoke Park Junior School

Two Voices

As the air raid passed by, the swooping owls glide
in the misty sky.
The sound of the sirens screaming as the beautiful moon
appears out of the blue night sky.
Running into the cold shelter, hearing sirens ringing
through the families' ears.
The teenagers are fighting for their lives as the children
are evacuated from the city.
Guns firing through the air, like exploding fireworks.

Samantha Williams (10)
Stoke Park Junior School

I Am The Lion

I am the lion . . . with a calm and controlled temper.
I am the lion . . . with claws as sharp as daggers.
I am the lion . . . I silently survey my prey.
I am the lion . . . brave and mighty.
I am the lion . . . I sneak and growl.
I am the lion . . . I'm grand, I'm fierce.

Thomas Moorcroft (10)
Stoke Park Junior School

Two Voices

Lovely lavender blowing in the peaceful countryside
but toxic gas is steaming towards London.
As small fluffy snow falls down on Christmas Eve,
the bombs start falling like hailstones.
As gigantic exploding bombs go off, the pretty colourful
fireworks still go on.
As the blood streams from bodies, there is still
a peaceful orange sunset.

Mitchell Shilling (10)
Stoke Park Junior School

Zebra

I am the zebra . . . my black and white stripes let me blend
into the landscape.
I am the zebra . . . my golden yellow eyes shimmering
in the sunlight.
I am the zebra . . . I'm big, friendly and I won't hurt you.
I am the zebra . . . I may be big but I'm scared,
I'm scared by tigers.
I am the zebra . . . when I run my tail swings round.

Shea Manning (9)
Stoke Park Junior School

Monkey

I am a monkey who's brave and broad.
I am a monkey who's bronze like a coin.
I am a monkey with blue gorgeous eyes.
I am a monkey, my ears are like huge biscuits.
I am a monkey, the cheekiest of them all.
I am a monkey who's got the silliest smile of all.
I am a monkey, my nose is as wet as the river.
I am a monkey, my hair is so scruffy.

Connor Gregory (10)
Stoke Park Junior School

The Cheetah

I am the cheetah, the fastest of them all.
I am the cheetah, as strong as a charging bull.
I am the cheetah, intelligent and bright.
I am the cheetah and I am going to win the fight.
I am the cheetah with fur as soft as sand.
I am the cheetah with paws as big as a child's hand.
I am the cheetah with a very long tail.
I am the cheetah and I am a *male!*

Joshua Gissing (9)
Stoke Park Junior School

Wartime Poem

As the young went to fight to keep us free
like a leaf floating off the tree in the autumn wind
a bullet rushed past the skin, it was too late to turn back,
the war had started.
Another bullet and another hit.
The boy's body felt so empty, it was over.
The war had ended and so had the boy's life.

Jordon Hatton (10)
Stoke Park Junior School

Two Voices

As there are heaping bodies on the floor, men sleep in their beds.
People's homes shattered and shredded while others' homes
are standing and free.
As air raids dropped bombs, joyful owls are screaming
in the trees.
Bits of bomb scattered, while fireworks are exploding
in the gleaming sky.

Daisy Jones (10)
Stoke Park Junior School

The Crocodile

There is a huge cruel crocodile living by the tropical sea,
Today he might find you and pounce, so how scared you will be.
As he walks past you will gaze upon his sharp teeth
like swords ready to kill,
That old scary crocodile has a very scaly back.
Before you know it that crocodile shall . . . *bite!*
That's a monster don't you think?

Emma Kane (9)
Stoke Park Junior School

I Am The Lion

I am the lion . . . with my blood-red eyes.
I am the lion . . . with teeth as sharp as carving knives.
I am the lion . . . who roars the loudest of them all.
I am the lion . . . with my golden mane as shiny as a block of gold.
I am the lion . . . who approaches my prey with extreme caution.
I am the lion . . . who rules the African Savannah.
I am the lion . . . who rules the world.

Callum Ward (9)
Stoke Park Junior School

Elephant

I am an elephant lying around on the rough ground.
I am an elephant, big and strong,
I help tow friends when I come along.
I am an elephant with two big ears shaped like two protractors.
I am an elephant with skin of grey,
when I'm in the water I shine.
I am an elephant with great big horns like vampire teeth.

Hayden Doust (9)
Stoke Park Junior School

Giraffe

I am the giraffe with eyes as black as night.
I am the giraffe with eyes on the side of my cream-coloured face.
I am the giraffe whose ears lean towards sound.
I am the giraffe with my yellow and brown neck.
I am the giraffe, the king of camouflage with a super long neck for spotting prey.
I am the giraffe, taller than a skyscraper.

Samuel Gray (10)
Stoke Park Junior School

The Ostrich!

I am the ostrich, the dinosaur seen today.
I am the flightless bird, are you not amazed?
I have the feathers as black as a big moon.
I have the roundest eyes that will always start to gloom.
I have the slimmest neck as thin as it could be.
I have the cutest legs and that's how you'll be me.
The ostrich!

Deanne Sara Smith (9)
Stoke Park Junior School

Jaguar

I am the jaguar with a nose as dark as the night sky.
I am the jaguar with sparkling golden eyes.
I am the jaguar with the strongest jaws.
I am the jaguar with painted on spots.
I am the jaguar with silky smooth fur.
I am the jaguar with the longest whiskers.
I am the jaguar that runs as fast as a car.

Lucas Bright (9)
Stoke Park Junior School

Lion

I am the lion, my mane is the shining golden sun.
I am the lion, my whiskers are like new, sharp, shiny needles.
I am the lion, my eyes are like two gold stars.
I am the lion, my paws are like brand new padding.
I am the lion, my nose is like dark mud.
I am the lion, my fur is like new golden thread.

Elena Beckett-Oxenham (9)
Stoke Park Junior School

I Am The Meerkat

I am the meerkat . . . cunningly looking for predators.
I am the meerkat . . . I secretly live underground.
I am the meerkat . . . deviously looking for scorpions to eat.
I am the meerkat . . . small as a beaver.
I am the meerkat . . . sly as an eagle.
I am the meerkat . . . as fast as a cheetah.

Callan Winstanley (9)
Stoke Park Junior School

I Am The Mighty Lion

I am the mighty lion with eyes red like the Devil's blood,
I am the fearless lion, my mane is like a squirrel's big bushy tail.
I am a warrior with teeth as sharp as a hundred pointy knives.
I am a vicious lion with my nose so wet and cold,
I am the lion, that is my name,
I am the lion, roaring is my game.

Sally Waite (9)
Stoke Park Junior School

The Snake

All hail before me!
My deadly beady eyes like space
Camouflaged skin protects me from enemies
My twister tongue flickers through blistered black lips
All cried.

Luke Spring (9)
Stoke Park Junior School

Zebra

I am a zebra, my stripes are like good and bad.
I am a zebra, my eyes are like black jewels.
I am a zebra, my nose is like thick mud.
I am a zebra, my hair is like grass in a meadow.
I am a zebra, my legs are as thin as pencils.

Jake Haysom (9)
Stoke Park Junior School

The Lion

I am the lion with fur as thick as wool.
I am the lion with eyes as dark as coal.
I am the lion with ears as pointy as mountains.
I am the lion with teeth as white as pearls.

Jack Bird (9)
Stoke Park Junior School

Hallowe'en

Bone cracker
Blood scarer
Slow dripper
Haunted spiders
Spooky ghosts
Red blooded eyes
Children scarer
Witches slimer
Candle water
Silver skeletons
Moon dancer
Slime lover
Jumpy drippers
Haunted candy men
Ghost dribbler
Children snatcher
Haunted bones
Spooky spiders
Blood drinker
Ghost dancer
Haunted skeletons
Ghost dribbler
Red blooded dancers
Children skeletons
Witch scarer
Candle maker
Skeleton lovers
Moon snatcher
Moon lover
Jumpy ghosts
Haunted dribblers
Cat frightener.

Hayley Winstanley (10)
Trosnant Junior School

Tornado

The tornado
twisting
and
spinning
the whole
wide world
around
like
a
twisting
spinning
and
spinning
and
spinning
around
the
universe
eating
up all
that's
around
it.

Bradley Luke Rance (9)
Trosnant Junior School

Happiness

Happiness is smiley people and is the colour blue.
Happiness smells like soap and feels like a soft and silky pillow.
Happiness tastes like a roast dinner
and sounds like people having fun.
Happiness puts a smile on your face.
Happiness is great.

Kyisha Hansler (9)
Trosnant Junior School

Hallowe'en

Blood dripper
Ghost scarer
Child screamer
Bone crusher
Spooky spider
Moon lover
Skeleton dancer
Candle holder
Haunted nightmares
Pumpkin squasher
Sour sweets
Soul keeper
Shocking witches
Heart breaker
Frightening thriller
Child grabber
Party ruiner
Wicked witches
Candy taker
Giggling ghost
Pumpkin lighter.

Meg Skinner (10)
Trosnant Junior School

Anger

I'm red
And tense
And sharp
I'm out of
Control
I like spice
I am loud
And bumpy
I've got rage!

Tyler Allen (9)
Trosnant Junior School

Hallowe'en

Blood dripper
Sweetie taker
Bone cruncher
Scary maker
Soul taker
Slime trailer
Children scarer
Ghost hunter
Shadow creeper
Fancy dresser
White flower
Body shiver
Jumping spider
Ghost spooker
Axe holder
Zombie killer
Good flyer
Mummy creeper
Body wrapper
Dark shiver
Bone breaker.

Natasha Richardson (10)
Trosnant Junior School

Winter

Winter is cool
Winter is tough
When it comes to winter, it's rough
You're my snow angel from Heaven
To come down and comfort me
You're the right person for me
You're my baby girl and you always will be
So go off and have some fun without me.

Lennox Ryan Moore (11)
Trosnant Junior School

Hallowe'en

Skeleton hanger
Creepy dreamer
Shocking sleepwalker
Pumpkin lighter
Sweet eater
Little squealer
Child scarer
Spider biter
Ghoul hater
Soul snatcher
Coffin creeper
Floorboard creaker
Scary shaker
Blood dripper
Bone breaker
Horrible monster
Grave riser
Broomstick riser
Rat eater
Light flicker.

Kate Pearce (10)
Trosnant Junior School

Monkeys

Cheeky chimps
Tree swinger
Nut eater
Banana muncher
Funky browner
Hairy leaper
Bottom shower
Vegetable nibbler
Water hater
Mum lover.

Liberty Gordon (10)
Trosnant Junior School

Hallowe'en

Pumpkin carver
Blood dripper
Children scarer
Door squeaker
Grave riser
Soul taker
Skeleton waker
Broomstick rider
People freaker
Spooky spider
Ghost hater
Spook maker
Window smasher
Wet creator
Fancy dress styler
Creepy sleepover.

Grace Shepherd (10)
Trosnant Junior School

Scarecrow

Crow scarer
Seed protector
Farm lover
Straw maker
Jumble wearer
Hay cuffs
Stick framer
Bird nester
Friend needer
Tractor avoider
Mask wearer
Wood frame.

Arron Peter Gooderham (11)
Trosnant Junior School

The Seasons

Spring

S plashing in the windy, wet rain
P utting flowers into the earth
R unning through the puddles
I n and out of the garden
N ever-ending smells of the flowers in spring
G ardens smelling lovely.

Summer

S wimming pool out all month
U nder the sea, swimming away
M aking fun all month
M usic on all day
E veryone having fun
R unning on the field, playing away.

Caitlin Hunter (11)
Trosnant Junior School

Robots

R obots are very powerful
O pening his shiny control panels
B reaks metal objects
O pening his shiny battery
T iny fast legs
S trange eyes like screws.

Brandon Moore (11)
Trosnant Junior School

Hallowe'en

I love Hallowe'en
Like rats, like blood
Like skeletons, like dancing
Like ghosts, like haunting
Like children, like trick or treating
I love Hallowe'en.

Owen Larkin (10)
Trosnant Junior School

Happiness

Happiness is yellow because it is the same colour as the sun,
The sun is warm like happiness.
Happiness tastes like candyfloss
Because candyfloss vanishes just like happiness,
One minute people are happy and then they're not.

Kira Bravington (9)
Trosnant Junior School

Urban Town Senses

The colour of a blue car in an urban town.
The smell of jam doughnuts in an urban town.
The look of bare trees in an urban town.
I feel lots of leaves crunching around my feet in an urban town.
The sound of honking cars and buses in an urban town.

Curtis Tait (9)
Trosnant Junior School

Poetry Explorers 2009 - Hampshire Poets

Young Writers Information

We hope you have enjoyed reading this book - and that you will continue to enjoy it in the coming years.

If you like reading and writing poetry drop us a line, or give us a call, and we'll send you a free information pack.

Alternatively if you would like to order further copies of this book or any of our other titles, then please give us a call or log onto our website at www.youngwriters.co.uk.

Young Writers Information
Remus House
Coltsfoot Drive
Peterborough
PE2 9JX
(01733) 890066